MW01065060

Connecting the Dots

From Prophecy to Messiah

Mary Christian

All Bible scriptures were taken from KJV

WestBow Press books may be ordered through booksellers or by contacting:

WestBow Press
A Division of Thomas Nelson & Zondervan
1663 Liberty Drive
Bloomington, IN 47403
www.westbowpress.com
1 (866) 928-1240

ISBN: 978-1-9736-5181-9 (sc)
ISBN: 978-1-9736-5183-3 (hc)
ISBN: 978-1-9736-5182-6 (e)

Library of Congress Control Number: 2019900823

Print information available on the last page.

WestBow Press rev. date: 01/30/2019

This book is dedicated to my mother,
who believed that I could!

Much gratitude to Karen Potter Murphy,
Author of Higden … A Place in the Heart.
I am so grateful for her encouragement and help.

Contents

Preface

Connecting the Dots is a daily devotional collection and Bible study that aspires to help us remember the events and lessons surrounding the crucifixion and resurrection of Jesus Christ. The twenty-seven devotionals weave together scripture from the Old and New Testaments, especially as they pertain to Old Testament prophecy and New Testament fulfillment of prophecy concerning our Messiah and Redeemer.

It is important and necessary to first read the "Bible Readings" to thoroughly understand the author's devotional thoughts. The author's thoughts are from the heart, but only God's Word has the power to effect change in our lives. The author recommends beginning the devotionals about twenty-one days before Resurrection Sunday.

This book was written by a layperson, without formal education in theology or journalism. Without the deeper knowledge of theology, the author writes with reverence and awe. Yet, to know God even on an elementary level opens our minds to concepts that are profound and large and rich. So we write with the intent to honor God, strengthen fellow believers, and hopefully, bring unbelievers to Christ.

Part I

The Divine Plan

Introduction

The Sovereign God

> Thus saith the Lord the King of Israel, and
> his redeemer the Lord of hosts;
> I am the first, and I am the last; and
> beside me there is no God.
> I am God, and there is none else; I am God, and
> there is none like me. (Isaiah 44:6; 46:9)

We cannot, in our earthly, finite minds, completely comprehend God:

> For my thoughts are not your thoughts, neither are your ways my ways, saith the Lord. For as the heavens are higher than the earth, so are my ways higher than your ways, and my thoughts than your thoughts. (Isaiah 55:8–9)

The one and only God, the Almighty Creator, spoke, and the universe that was formed in His infinite and creative mind became physical reality.

> In the beginning God created the heaven and the earth. And the earth was without form, and void; and darkness was upon the face of the deep. And the Spirit of God moved upon the face of the waters. And God said, "Let there be … !" (Genesis 1:1–3)

Could it be that the first five "creation days" were primarily preparation of the habitat for what God considered His preeminent and predominant creation?

> God said, "Let us make man in our image, after our likeness: and let them have dominion over the fish… and over the fowl… and over the cattle, and over all the earth… every… thing that creepeth upon the earth." So God created man in his own image, in the image of God created he him; male and female created he them. (Genesis 1:26–27)

Then God delegated authority to man.

> God blessed them, and God said unto them, "Be fruitful, and multiply… replenish the earth,

and subdue it... have dominion over... every living thing." (Genesis 1:28)

Oh, the depth of the riches both of the
wisdom and knowledge of God!
How unsearchable are his judgments,
and his ways past finding out!
Who hath known the mind of the Lord?
Or who hath been his counsellor?
For of him, and through him, and to him, are all things.
To whom be glory forever! Amen. (Romans 11:33–34, 36)

The Divine Plan

Bible Readings: Psalm 8, 139:1–18

God the Father

Early in Scripture God identified Himself as a Father when He referred to Israel as His firstborn (Exodus 4:22). In the best of familial situations, the term *father* brings feelings of endearment and respect, as well as imagery of strength and honor. Good fathers provide stability, guidance, protection, provision, discipline, and love for the family. So the knowledge that God is our heavenly Father is a sensible correlation to those who have or had good fathers.

Moses referred to God as *Ab* (Hebrew transliteration, meaning "father, source, and inventor"), from which comes *Abba* (New Testament Aramaic for "father"). Moses wrote, "Is not he thy father… hath he not made thee?" (Deuteronomy 32:6). Isaiah wrote, "Thou, O Lord, art our father, our redeemer; thy name is from everlasting" (Isaiah 63:16). Jesus Himself referred to God the Father as *Abba* (Mark 14:36). If one has problems conceptualizing God as a father, the following passages given through Old Testament prophets reveal the heart of God. Listen as God speaks with love, compassion, protection, and guidance—truly a lesson in fatherhood.

> I am the Lord thy God which teacheth thee … leadeth thee by the way that thou shouldest go. (Isaiah 48:17)

> [Though a mother may forget her child] I [will] not forget thee. Behold, I have graven thee upon the palms of my hands; thy walls are continually before me. (Isaiah 49:15, 16)

> I have loved thee with an everlasting love: therefore with loving-kindness have I drawn thee. (Jeremiah 31:3)

> I will cause them to walk by the rivers of waters in a straight way, wherein they shall not stumble: for I am a father to Israel. (Jeremiah 31:9)

> The Lord thy God in [your] midst … is mighty… will rejoice over thee with joy… will rest [you] in his love… will joy over thee with singing. (Zephaniah 3:17)

God is, indeed, a loving Father who delights in all of His children. When we contemplate the magnitude of that love, we can marvel with David. "What is man, that thou art mindful of him?… hast crowned him with glory and honour. Thou madest him to have dominion over the works of thy hands; thou hast put all things under his feet" (Psalm 8:4–6). How amazing that we are so honored!

Conversely, when we *fail* to reflect the Father's glory, we might ask in embarrassment, "What is man, that thou shouldest magnify him… set thine heart upon him… visit him every morning, and try him every moment?" (Job 7:17–18). And fail we will, because since the fall of man in the garden of Eden, sin is inherent in humankind.

The fact that His beloved creation would disappoint and disobey did not, however, come as a surprise to the eternal, omniscient God. He knew the end from the very beginning! "I am God… declaring the end from the beginning, and from ancient times the things that are not yet done" (Isaiah 46:9–10). He knew when He was forming the universe as our habitat that we would sin. He knew before time began that He would have to redeem us. Because of this, the Redeemer, who would be sacrificed to atone for our sins, was virtually "slain from the foundation of the world" (Revelation 13:8).

Since God knew before the creation of man that we would sin and how costly our redemption would be, we might wonder *why* He created man. Surely the reason was the same yearning that inspires human desire to have children—a yearning to love, fellowship, and nurture our own offspring. He placed within our hearts a bit of His heart when He blessed Adam and Eve, and told them to be fruitful and increase in number (Genesis 1:28).

In procreation we hope to see in our offspring our own best attributes. We train our children to have an appreciation for the issues of life that we, as adults, consider important. Yet we take great pride in their distinctive individuality. Loving parents have high hopes for their children to become the best they can achieve in character and personality. Humanity is flawed, however, and sin is in our nature. Yet when we see our children err, we do not love them less. On the contrary, we correct, we instruct, and we encourage with the greatest of love. Often it is necessary to forgive. Sometimes it is necessary to chasten. Always, the effort to redeem is worthwhile.

God our heavenly Father is merciful and forgiving. God the Father promised for sinful humankind a sinless Redeemer. He promised for His disoriented children a Prophet to lead them. He promised for those lacking justice a righteous Judge. God promised those who were oppressed a righteous King. And to all who are in need, God sent His faithful Servant. All of those positions could only be fulfilled by and through one man—the only sinless man—God's Son. God incarnate, the promised Messiah, was and is the only one who qualified to fill these needs! How would that take place?

God lovingly gave His Word to inform us of His plan. God, the absolute Author, wrote His love letter to humanity with many hands and many quills. He eloquently wrote the past and the future using metaphor, simile, personification, and antithesis. His book is history, geography, muniment, ancestry, biography, drama, romance, mystery, and instruction. His book has the power to cause one to weep and to laugh, the power to reprove and to restore.

The Holy Spirit of God, who was present at the creation and the immaculate conception of Jesus Messiah, our Redeemer, Prophet, Judge, King, and Servant, not only lives in the hearts of those redeemed, but also lives in the words of God's book. It is He who quickens alive this Word in our hearts as we read and experience weeping turning to laughter and conviction turning to joy.

God's book has one main purpose, that being the story of His love for the Jews and the gentiles proven by His plan of salvation and redemption through His Son Incarnate. In His love story, God foretells His redemptive plan by weaving through His book from Genesis to Revelation, like a scarlet ribbon, the announcement of whom and what to expect as salvation. God used direct and forthright words that were unmistakable signs. He used human prophets to give this information of things to come so we would know. God also used many prefigurative signs (foreshadowing), so that students of His book would be alert to recognize the clues as prophecy unfolded. (i.e., Genesis 22 and Isaiah 7:14, with chapters 8–9) Truly He wanted us to study His book in every generation looking for the next event in this great love story.

Connecting the Dots

- Deuteronomy 18:15
- Isaiah 11:1–4
- Isaiah 42:1
- Isaiah 59:20
- Jeremiah 23:5, 6

The Divine Plan

Bible Readings: Isaiah 40:1–11

Revealing the Son

"Messiah, the Prince" (Daniel 9:25), was to be greatly anticipated. Prophets of old had been given clues to identify Him, and the Jewish people were to be alert, watching and eagerly awaiting. Greater than earthly royalty, the Messiah was to be deity, pre-identified by a star (Numbers 24:17)! He would be the "Mighty God," possessing all power (Isaiah 9:6), who was from everlasting to everlasting—the "Ancient of Days" (Daniel 7:9, 22). Through Messiah all things were created in heaven and earth, whether they are visible or invisible. It is through Messiah's will and power that all things hold together. He has supremacy (Colossians 1:13–18)!

Through Messiah the kingdom of God, a holy kingdom, would be established. Followers of the Messiah would be a part of this kingdom in which He is "King" (Zechariah 9:9); a part of His spiritual body, of which He is "Head" (Ephesians 4:15); a part of His church/temple, of which He is "Chief Cornerstone" (Ephesians 2:20); and built on the foundation established by the prophets and apostles. He would be "Wonderful," "Counselor" and their "Prince of Peace" (Isaiah 9:6).

Messiah would be the agent through which the covenant would be fulfilled and accomplished. That covenant would be for the purpose of redeeming fallen humanity. Through the Messiah, "The Lord our Righteousness," would come righteous perfection that would cover human sin (Jeremiah 23:6), because He would be the "Holy One" (Psalm 16:10) and the "Lamb of God," sacrificed for our sins (John 1:29).

How did God's divine plan for redemption unfold?

> And in the sixth month the angel Gabriel was sent from God unto a city of Galilee, named Nazareth, To a virgin espoused to a man whose name was Joseph, of the house of David; and the virgin's name was Mary. And the angel came in unto her, and said, "Hail, thou that art highly favoured, the Lord is with thee: blessed art thou among women." And when she saw him, she was troubled at his saying, and cast in her mind what manner of salutation this should be. And the angel said unto her, "Fear not, Mary: for thou hast found favour with God. And, behold, thou shalt conceive in thy womb, and bring forth a son, and shalt call his name Jesus. He shall be great, and shall be called the Son of the Highest: and the Lord God shall

give unto him the throne of his father David: And he shall reign over the house of Jacob for ever; and of his kingdom there shall be no end." Then said Mary unto the angel, "How shall this be, seeing I know not a man?" And the angel answered and said unto her, "The Holy Ghost shall come upon thee, and the power of the Highest shall overshadow thee: therefore also that holy thing which shall be born of thee shall be called the Son of God." (Luke 1:26–35)

Now the birth of Jesus Christ was on this wise: When as his mother Mary was espoused to Joseph, before they came together, she was found with child of the Holy Ghost. Then Joseph her husband, being a just man, and not willing to make her a public example, was minded to put her away privily. But while he thought on these things, behold, the angel of the Lord appeared unto him in a dream, saying, "Joseph, thou son of David, fear not to take unto thee Mary thy wife: for that which is conceived in her is of the Holy Ghost. And she shall bring forth a son, and thou shalt call his name Jesus: for he shall save his people from their sins." Now all this was done, that it might

> be fulfilled which was spoken of the Lord by the prophet, saying, "Behold, a virgin shall be with child, and shall bring forth a son, and they shall call his name Emmanuel, which being interpreted is, God with us." Then Joseph being raised from sleep did as the angel of the Lord had bidden him, and took unto him his wife: And knew her not till she had brought forth her firstborn son: and he called his name JESUS. (Matthew 1:18–25)

Psalm 2 was considered to be a royal psalm, composed for the coronation of kings. It is also considered to be a Messianic psalm. Under the inspiration of God the Father, the psalmist wrote prophetically concerning the anticipated Messiah, God incarnate. God the Father declared: "Thou art my Son; this day have I begotten thee. Ask of me, and I shall give thee… the uttermost parts of the earth for thy possession" (Psalm 2:7–8). Jesus confirmed His authority, declaring that all things had been committed to Him by the Father (Matthew 28:18). Jesus is and will be sovereign over all nations (Hebrews 1:2). He declared Himself to be the "Almighty" (Revelation 1:8). He declared Himself to be the way to God, the revelation of truth, and our only means to eternal life (John 14:6).

The omniscient Lord did not come to earth with misconceptions about His incarnation or His life on earth. The eternal Son of God knew since the "foundation of the world" (Revelation 13:8) His purpose and time frame to serve humanity. He knew the quality of life He would experience. He knew He had a social, emotional, and physical cross to bear. Jesus's earthly parents were godly but humble in status. There was neither majesty nor grandeur for the birth of the King of Kings. Though all of heaven celebrated, His birth was not heralded with pomp and circumstance by earthly royalty. He was born, according to Bible translations, in a stable. According to scripture, Jesus was placed, because of the exigency of the situation, in an animal-feeding trough for a cradle.

From His birth to His death, Jesus experienced rejection. Scripture does not reveal much from His childhood, but we can imagine that He might have been ostracized as an "illegitimate" child. Matthew 13:53–57 notes that Jesus did not do many miracles when He ministered in Nazareth, His hometown, because of their unbelief. In verse 58 Jesus then acknowledged that a prophet is not without honor except in his own country or his own house. John 7:5 notes that Jesus's biological half-brothers did not believe in Him (until later, perhaps after the resurrection).

Superficial humanity is biased toward beauty. From then until now, beauty is lifted up in importance and treated as an indication of worth. Jesus appears from scripture not to have had a handsome physical appearance. Long before Jesus was born, Isaiah wrote prophetically concerning Jesus as the root of Jesse:

> To whom is the arm of the Lord revealed? For he shall grow up before him as a tender plant…he hath no form nor comeliness; and when we shall see him, there is no beauty that we should desire him. He is despised and rejected of men; a man of sorrows, and acquainted with grief: and we hid as it were our faces from him; he was despised, and we esteemed him not. Surely he hath borne our griefs, and carried our sorrows: yet we did esteem him stricken, smitten of God, and afflicted. (Isaiah 53:1–4)

A couple of decades after Jesus physically left the earth, Paul wrote to the Colossians (1:26) describing Jesus Christ as "the mystery of God." To the church in Rome (Romans 16:25–26), he wrote that Jesus was the mystery hidden for long ages but now revealed. He went on to tell the Colossian church that in Christ is hidden all the treasures of wisdom and knowledge. Those treasures are available and attainable by all who seek Christ Jesus.

Contemplate the miracle! Divinity permeating humanity to enshrine and provide a Savior! God sent His own immaculate Son to redeem sinful humankind! Simply communicated, God is love. Thus, the greatest record of the Father's love for all of humankind is succinctly recorded in John 3:16: "For God so loved the world that he gave his only begotten Son, that whosoever believeth in him should not perish, but have everlasting life."

Connecting the Dots

- Isaiah 7:14

The Divine Plan

Bible Readings: Matthew 3:13–17, 17:1–6; John 5:31–39

God the Son—Fulfilling Prophecy

Proverbs 25:2 presents a challenge. "It is the glory of God to conceal a thing: but the honour of kings is to search out a matter." We understand that we are to be students of God's Word, searching for all that is rich in wisdom, positively life-changing, and prophetic. If the students of scripture in Jesus's day had been attentive, they might have connected the dots relating prophetic scripture with the anticipated Messiah. Then they might have realized Jesus's embodiment of those prophecies. Consider just a few of the most well-known among hundreds of Messianic prophecies and how they were fulfilled at Jesus's birth.

The prophet Isaiah gave a clue as to what to expect at the coming of this ruler: a child of virgin birth who would Himself be God living among humanity (Isaiah 7:14). The prophet Micah prophesied that the town of Bethlehem should expect to be birthplace of one who would rule over Israel (Micah 5:2). The prophecies of Zechariah, Isaiah, and Jeremiah confirm that the child would come from the genealogy of Judah, Jesse, and David. Matthew 1 gives us the genealogy of Jesus, confirming that He descended from

Abraham, as promised by God, through Judah, Jesse, and David (Jeremiah 33:14–15).

It is noteworthy that woven into Jesus's human family tapestry were typical people, many of whom were well known—some for their virtue and some for their sinful nature. Doubtless, all of them struggled in the universal battle between righteousness and unrighteousness. Many of them had flagrant moral or intrinsic issues; yet from today's perspective, we call many of them godly and blessed. Take a look at just a few of Jesus's human ancestors whose names are very familiar.

Among those listed in the genealogy is Jacob, who used lies and trickery to steal his brother's birthright. Judah, lacking integrity, was tricked by his daughter-in-law into fathering her son, Perez. Boaz was born to the union of Salmon with a prostitute named Rahab from the idolatrous nation of Canaan. Boaz married Ruth, a woman from Moab, the nation that originated from the incest of Lot with his daughters. King David fathered Solomon with Bathsheba, the wife of Uriah, a man whose demise David arranged. Solomon, though known for his wisdom, "loved many foreign women" besides his first wife, Pharaoh's daughter (1 Kings 11:1). In fact, he had seven hundred wives and three hundred concubines, certainly a stretch for "one flesh!" (Genesis 2:24)

Lots of skeletons in the proverbial closet and lots of dirt swept under the proverbial rug! Family members of whom to be ashamed and family members of whom to be proud, they certainly substantiate the fact that everyone needs a savior. And Jesus is the Savior for all nations. How benevolent for the immaculate and sovereign Lord to humble Himself to be born to sinful man! Jesus, "Who, being in the form of God… made Himself of no reputation… being found in fashion as a man, he humbled Himself." (Philippians 2:6–8)

Scripture tells us of certain individuals who were watchful for the long-awaited Messiah and alert to the Holy Spirit's revelation of Jesus when He was born. The priest, Zechariah, and his wife, Elizabeth, were certainly expecting the birth of the Christ, because it had been revealed to them concerning their son, John. John the Baptist, as he came to be known, was born when they were well along in years after an angel presaged his birth and purpose to Zechariah. John's purpose was to be an evangelist, announcing the arrival and ministry of the long-expected Messiah and preparing the hearts of people to receive the Christ (Luke 1:13–17).

Shepherds tending sheep in the fields near Bethlehem received and responded to divine, angelic notice of the Messiah's arrival (Luke 2:8–15).

The Magi recognized the magnitude of the event. Possibly gentiles from Persia, they may have been astronomers, because it appears their expertise was in charting the courses and events of the heavenly bodies. They were obviously aware of the prophecy concerning the significance of a star (or perhaps conjunction of heavenly bodies) that related to and announced the birth of a king (Matthew 2; Numbers 24:17).

Simeon, a righteous and devout man from Jerusalem, had revelation from the Holy Spirit that Jesus was the anticipated salvation and glory to the people of Israel, as well as to the gentiles (Luke 2:25–32).

The prophetess Anna, on the arrival of Mary and Joseph bringing Jesus to the temple in Jerusalem to offer sacrifice, "gave thanks likewise unto the Lord, and spake of him to all them that looked for redemption in Jerusalem" (Luke 2:36–38).

Paul, an apostle of Jesus, wrote in retrospect, "When the fulness of time was come, God sent forth his Son, made of a woman, made under the law, to redeem them that were under the law, that we might receive the adoption of sons" (Galatians 4:4–5). In God's chosen timing, Jesus was born to a virgin, who miraculously conceived of God through the Holy Spirit (Luke 1–2). He was Son of God and Son of man.

Jesus's ethnic diversity substantiates His true humanity. Jesus's virgin birth, miraculous power, and fulfillment of prophecies are evidence of His true divinity.

Revelation and Affirmation by God the Father

God the Father revealed Jesus as Son and Messiah at His birth with the prophetic star for all in the East to see, and with the angelic announcement to shepherds (Luke 2).

God the Father revealed Jesus as His Son on the occasion of Jesus's baptism in water as an adult. He spoke audibly from heaven, declaring, "This is My Son." The sinless Son of God submitted Himself to the public rite of baptism, thereby identifying Himself with humankind and human sinfulness. In doing so, He set an example to all who would follow Him, describing His participation as "fulfilling all righteousness." Water baptism became a fundamental rite for Christianity, representing death to sin and resurrection in Christ. This was pleasing to the Father, and in this holy scene, we recognize the presence of the triune God—Father, Son, and Holy Spirit (Matthew 3). The apostle John's gospel recorded John the Baptist's revelation of Jesus.

> The next day John seeth Jesus coming unto him, and saith, "Behold the Lamb of God which taketh away the sin of the world. This

> is he of whom I said, 'After me cometh a man which is preferred before me: for he was before me.' And I knew him not: but that he should be made manifest to Israel, therefore am I come baptizing with water." And John bare record, saying, "I saw the Spirit descending from heaven like a dove, and it abode upon him … He that sent me to baptize with water … said … 'Upon whom thou shalt see the Spirit descending, and remaining on him, the same is he which baptizeth with the Holy Ghost." (John 1:29–34)

God the Father again revealed Jesus as His Son at the transfiguration. Jesus was seen by the apostles Peter, James, and John in a brilliant and glorious manifestation. Having accompanied Jesus up a high mountain to pray, the three apostles witnessed that as Jesus was praying, the appearance of His face changed, and His clothing became a bright and glistening white (Luke 9:29). On this occasion Jesus was seen by the three apostles as He was conversing with Moses and Elias (Elijah). (This also was revelation to the apostles who had never seen Elijah or Moses, who lived hundreds of years before them.) Luke's gospel reveals that the three of them spoke of Jesus's approaching death (Luke 9). (See also 2 Peter 1:12–18.)

Affirmation by God the Son

Likewise, Jesus revealed God as Father. In His teachings, for example, Jesus said our good deeds should be done to glorify the Father. Jesus taught His followers to pray to the Father. He gave credit to the Father for tender care for the birds and provision for all creation. Jesus referred to the synagogue as His Father's house. Jesus explained that He came to earth to do the will of His Father in heaven. Jesus said that whatever He heard from the Father is what He conveyed to the people. Finally, on the cross, Jesus asked God the Father to forgive those who crucified Him and to receive His spirit as He died.

Jesus identified Himself as God's Son and the promised Redeemer to His hometown of Nazareth. At the synagogue in Nazareth He read the promise of the Messianic Servant from Isaiah 61. "The Spirit of the Lord is upon me… He hath anointed me… He hath sent me…" On concluding this reading, He rolled up the scroll, sat down, and said, "This day is this scripture fulfilled in your ears" (Luke 4:16–21).

Jesus affirmed His divine identity to His Jewish opposition. "Search the scriptures; for in them ye think ye have eternal life: and they are they which testify of me" (John 5:39). "For had ye believed Moses, ye would have believed me" (John 5:46).

On the evening prior to His crucifixion, Jesus continued to reveal His relationship with the heavenly Father in the discussions at His final meal with His apostles. No less than fifteen times (John 14–16), Jesus explained how closely connected He is to God the Father. "He that hath seen me hath seen the Father" (John 14:9). It was important to Jesus to communicate that "the world must know that I love the Father; and as the Father gave me commandment, even so I do" (John 14:31). "The Father, that dwelleth in me, he doeth the works" (John 14:10). Jesus encouraged the apostles to obey His commands in the same way Jesus had obeyed the Father. Jesus assured them that everything He learned from the Father He had revealed to them.

Connecting the Dots

- Genesis 49:8–10 (See also Genesis 12:3, 22:18, 17:19, 21:12; Numbers 24:17)
- Psalm 2:7–9
- Isaiah 49:5, 6
- Malachi 3:1; Isaiah 40:3–5
- John 3:35

The Divine Plan

Bible Readings: Jeremiah 31:31–34;
Matthew 5:17–18; Hebrews 10:1–14

God the Son—Fulfilling the Law

There are no words to describe, nor can we comprehend, the righteousness and holiness of God. In His perfection, He has conveyed through spoken and written words what we need to know to avoid breaking His laws of righteousness and offending His holiness. Breaking God's law is sin, punishable by death. He gave us the written Word in both the Old Covenant and New Covenant so that we might please Him, and so that our lives will be productive and blessed. Jesus Christ, who fulfills the law and provides forgiveness, gives us His righteousness to cover our sinfulness. Jesus said that we should obey the law of God. Our own righteous efforts are never good enough, however; so we must be covered by the righteousness of Christ.

As Christians, we can claim and be safe in the righteousness of Christ; yet giving our best efforts to conform to His precepts is an act of love, reverence, obedience, and conscientiousness. (See Matthew 19:17; Romans 6:15 with Romans 7:7; Luke 18:18–20; Hebrews 10:26–27.)

As parents, when we see our young children attempting to live by the family principles and house rules we have taught them, our hearts are made tender to those efforts; then mercy and grace are abundant to our offspring. Likewise with our heavenly Father. His discipline is for our good, bringing about good health, prosperity, joy, and peace. (See Psalm 94:12; Hebrews 12:9–10.)

In His Sermon on the Mount, Jesus told His followers, "Think not that I am come to destroy the law, or the prophets: I am not come to destroy, but to fulfill" (Matthew 5:17). When Jesus was asked by one of the Pharisees which law was most important, He responded, "Thou shalt love the Lord thy God with all thy heart, and with all thy soul, and with all thy mind. This is the *first* and great commandment. And the *second* is like unto it, Thou shalt love thy neighbor as thyself. On these two commandments hang all the law and the prophets" (Matthew 22:37–40).

Israel's *moral laws* pertained to the relationship of God's people to Himself and the relationship of His people to each other. Jesus taught all who would listen to obey these two greatest commandments. Jesus fulfilled the moral laws, proving His love for God the Father and for humanity. He did so by coming to earth and obediently completing the redemptive work assigned to Him by the Father.

> That the world may know that I love the Father; and as the Father gave me commandment, even so I do. (John 14:31)
>
> As the Father hath loved me, so have I loved you. (John 15:9)
>
> Greater love hath no man than this, that a man lay down his life for his friends. (John 15:13)

Israel's *ceremonial laws* pertaining to atonement for sin required blood sacrifices. It began at Passover with the slaughter of a lamb to deliver and save Israel (Exodus 12). It continued on God's command in Leviticus 4, again to make restitution for and save the Israelites. Under the old law, these sacrifices were administered through the Levitical priesthood. The method was only a temporary foreshadowing of the permanent and perfect solution for sin. There was, in fact, weakness in this temporary solution, that being human failure. These same priests who ministered to others needed sacrifices for their own sins, as all of humankind "have sinned and come short" of being righteous (Romans 3:23; Leviticus 4:3; 16:6; Hebrews 5:2, 3). Further, the priests, being human, were subject to death. Jesus, however, was sinless and lives forever, establishing a permanent priesthood, so He always lives to intercede on our behalf (Hebrews 7:24–25).

> If therefore perfection were by the Levitical priesthood... what further need was there that another priest should rise after the order of Melchizedek, and not be called after the order of Aaron? For he testifieth, "Thou art a priest forever, in the order of Melchizedek"... He was made priest... with an oath (when) the Lord sware and will not repent: "Thou art a priest forever." (Hebrews 7:11–17, 20–21; Psalm 110:4)

The sacrifice of animals gave no pleasure to God. When we observe the nearly human-like emotions God has created in many species of animals, we realize that the sacrifice of animals was most probably sorrowful to God (Matthew 10:29). The requirement of the sacrifice of animals for atonement speaks to us of the gravity of sin in the eyes and heart of God. God Himself spoke through the prophet Isaiah, "I delight not in the blood of bullocks, or of lambs, or... goats" (Isaiah 1:11). Under the old law, sacrifices for sin were offered continually and repeatedly because they were impermanent and imperfect. Jesus, however, became the final, permanent sacrifice for our sins. "For what the law could not do, in that it was weak through the flesh, God sending his own Son in the likeness of sinful flesh...

condemned sin … that the righteousness of the law might be fulfilled in us" (Romans 8:3–4).

> For the law having a shadow of good things to come, and not the very image of the things, can never with those sacrifices which they offered year by year continually make the comers thereunto perfect. For then would they not have ceased to be offered? Because that the worshippers once purged should have had no more conscience of sins. But in those sacrifices there is a remembrance again made of sins every year. For it is not possible that the blood of bulls and of goats should take away sins. Wherefore when he cometh into the world, he saith, "Sacrifice and offering thou wouldest not, but a body hast thou prepared me: In burnt offerings and sacrifices for sin thou hast had no pleasure." Then said I, "Lo, I come … to do thy will, O God" … By the which will we are sanctified through the offering of the body of Jesus Christ once for all. (From Hebrews 10:1–10; see Psalm 40:6–8.)

Jesus's sinless life and sacrificial death fulfilled and replaced the ceremonial laws, thereby permanently and perfectly satisfying the requirements for man's redemption.

Connecting the Dots

- Isaiah 1:11–20
- Psalm 51:16–17
- Leviticus 16:21–24
- Romans 3:23

The Divine Plan

Bible Readings: Luke 2:41–52; Matthew 4:23

God the Son—Passionate Teacher

We know details of the birth of Jesus, and we know the purpose of the emergency trip into Egypt (Matthew 2). After Herod's massacre of baby boys and his subsequent death, an angel of the Lord instructed Joseph in a dream to return with Mary and Jesus to Nazareth. Very little is written about the childhood of Jesus, yet we realize from the account in Luke 2 that God the Father was already in communication with His young Son. Jesus, as an early adolescent, was comfortable with the revered religious leaders. He was drawn to study, understanding, and discussion of the scriptures. Unintimidated, He found His place among the religious elites, listening and asking questions. Luke records that all who heard Him were amazed at His understanding and His answers to questions. Luke's gospel also notes that Jesus in His youth became strong in spirit, was filled with wisdom, and that the grace of God was upon Him (Luke 2:40).

As the "Messenger of the Covenant" and the "Counselor," Jesus came to teach and exemplify the loving heart of God the Father and to reveal the plan of salvation through Himself as the Messiah. He fulfilled the prophecies and brought the good news to the Jews first, and then to everyone who would believe (Romans 1:16). Jesus taught the masses (Matthew 5), and He taught one-on-one (Matthew 19:16). He taught priests in the synagogue (Matthew 4) and the immoral Samaritan woman (John 4). It was so natural for Him to explain and to instruct, and He did so out of love and not judgment (John 12:47–48).

We can hear compassion in the Teacher's words when He spoke to those needing direction. To the fishermen whose employment had become undependable and frustrating, He said, *If only* you will follow Me, I will give your life new meaning (Matthew 4:19). To the rich young ruler who felt a spiritual void and wanted a deeper sense of spiritual security, He said, *If only* you will "give... and follow me," you can reach perfection (Matthew 19:16–21). It is so amazing how completely He knew every individual—their personal history, their character flaws, their fears, and their spiritual needs. The omniscient Creator "came to His own," and He understood them thoroughly.

Jesus the Teacher now speaks divine guidance into our minds through His Word. He has a perfect plan for our individual lives, and He leads by His Holy Spirit. Every moment of your life and every breath you take, He is aware and involved as if you were His only child. He has a consuming passion for you as an individual. He knows your shortcomings and your fears. He knows your physical, spiritual, and emotional needs. He longs to strengthen your faith. He knows each of us thoroughly and yearns to bring His children to realize our need of Him as Savior.

Moreover, He wants each of us as individuals to realize our full potential as we come to understanding of, and are sanctified by, the Word (John 17:17). What is He speaking to you? What causes anguish within you? What gifting and talents has He created within you? What resources do you have? What preoccupies your mind? Are you alert to His voice?

Jesus longs to strengthen our faith, give us guidance, and teach us His ways. We learn from Him by living every moment in His presence, alert to His voice. Gently He leads us, saying, "Precious child, *if only* you would..." "One thing you lack, beloved..." "Choose the best, dear one."

Connecting the Dots

- Isaiah 9:6
- Malachi 3:1
- John 15:15

Part 2

Discussions at the Table

Introduction

Leading Up to the Last Supper

According to John 12, six days before Passover, Jesus arrived in Bethany, a village that was only two miles from Jerusalem. Jesus's friends—siblings Mary, Martha, and Lazarus, who lived in Bethany—attended a dinner that was given in Jesus's honor. During the evening Mary anointed Jesus with an expensive perfume. Knowing His death was imminent, Jesus confirmed her act of worship, saying that it was intended that she should save this perfume "against the day of my burying" (John 12:7).

The next day Jesus entered the City of Jerusalem to a royal reception. Arriving on a young donkey, He was welcomed by onlookers waving palms and shouting a Messianic blessing. "Hosanna to the Son of David: Blessed is he that cometh in the name of the Lord!" (Matthew 21:9). The prophet Zechariah had prophesied to Jerusalem to expect Messiah to enter the city humbly riding on a donkey (Zechariah 9:9). (The title "Son of David" was used when referring to the coming Messiah. The donkey was symbolic of humility and peace, but also of Davidic royalty.) Scripture records that His apostles did not understand this reception until after the resurrection. (See John 12:16.)

During the Passion Week, Jesus "cleansed" the temple, literally driving out those who were using the temple as a market. Jesus physically forced out vendors and buyers who were desecrating the House of God, saying, "It is written, 'My house shall be called the house of prayer,' but ye have made it a den of thieves" (Matthew 21:13). (See Isaiah 56:7; Jeremiah 7:11.)

During that week Jesus taught with parables on the Mount of Olives and taught in the temple. There He also responded to polemic debate concerning the scriptures, as He was challenged by the teachers of the law and Pharisees (Matthew 21–23). During the week of Passover, Jesus warned His followers of His impending death (John 12:23–33).

Jesus's arrival in Jerusalem was to complete His redeeming purpose—the institution of a new blood covenant, literally fulfilling the Passover. On Passover *He* would become the sacrificial Lamb. The old covenant was based on the blood of animals; the new covenant was based on the blood of Messiah. Isaiah prophesied and described how this divine ruler would function as the Suffering Servant, carrying out the will of God the Father as He established this new and permanent blood covenant. (See Isaiah 42, 49, 50, and 52. These chapters are replete with descriptions that betoken Christ's fulfillment of prophecy, for those who wish to "connect the dots.")

Passover began around sunset, and quite probably midweek that year. In the Father's sovereign, perfect timing, Jesus would have been crucified appropriately on Passover, the day on which the Paschal lamb was to be slaughtered in every Jewish household.

Jesus and the twelve apostles shared their last meal together, it would appear, on the evening before Passover. A private upper room and the wonderful fellowship that comes with sharing food created a comfortable atmosphere for Jesus to prepare the apostles for what laid ahead. From Jesus's lips that evening came teaching, encouragement, consolation, and warning for the group of men He had mentored to carry the gospel to the world. Jesus's words have been preserved and are still relevant today for all who would hear and believe His message and follow Him. Look deeper, now, into the important discussions that Jesus initiated at the dinner table that evening.

Discussions at the Table

Bible Reading: John 13:1–17

Humility and Servitude

Luke's record of their last supper that evening indicates that there was dispute among the apostles as to which of them would be greater when Jesus's kingdom was established (Luke 22:24). This shows how little they understood about the kingdom and how little, at that point, they had grasped of Jesus's teachings concerning serving others and humility. This was not the first time the apostles had argued over this issue. Earlier, responding to this same controversy, Jesus had illustrated with a little child that loving humility is greatness in God's eyes. "He that is least among you all—the same shall be great," He said (Luke 9:48). Mark 10 records a similar incident where brothers, James and John, asked for positions of authority in Jesus's coming kingdom. This prompted indignation among the others, requiring Jesus to explain again, "Whosoever of you will be the chiefest, shall be servant of all, for even the Son of Man did not come to be served, but to serve" (Mark 10:44–45).

Jesus expounded on humility at one point when teaching His apostles how they should perceive their duty as a servant of God. His illustration in Luke 17:7–10 of serving even a master who is demanding and ungrateful emphasizes the necessity of a heart that is humble. Jesus says that our attitude, even after having served sacrificially, should be, "We are unprofitable servants: we have done that which was our duty" (Luke 17:10).

On this unforgettable evening at their last supper, Jesus, the Master Teacher, again emphasized His lesson in humility and servitude. He did this by demonstration—washing the apostles' feet, as a servant might do in Jesus's era and culture. When He had finished His illustration, He asked, "Know ye what I have done to you? Ye call me Master and Lord: and ye say well; for so I am… I have given you an example, that ye should do as I have done to you" (John 13:12–15).

This was not the last lesson in humility and service that Jesus would demonstrate. His greatest illustration would follow within hours of the meal they shared that evening when He, as Servant of God, would humbly submit to torture and death on behalf of all of humanity. The lessons of servitude Jesus taught that evening are basic to His doctrine and necessary for all who would call themselves Christians, because in humble service we become illustrations of Jesus Christ for others to see.

A life of service develops humility, which enables us to assume the personality of Jesus. We can glimpse His personality and character from His self-description: "I am gentle and humble." Earlier Jesus had encouraged His followers to learn the discipline ("yoke") of humility. In this comforting verse

He offers to yoke Himself with us, lending assistance in our efforts to be like Him. The discipline and balance of humility, which goes hand-in-hand with gentleness, has an amazing benefit: peace that permeates the soul. "Come unto me, all ye that labour and are heavy laden, and I will give you rest. Take my yoke upon you, and learn of me; for I am meek and lowly in heart: and ye shall find rest unto your souls" (Matthew 11:28–29). When we have the humility and gentleness of the Lamb, we become like Him—endearing and approachable. (See Isaiah 53:7; John 1:29.)

Admittedly, we are comforted somewhat by the fact that these men who eventually evangelized and changed the world with the gospel needed to have a lesson repeated. This lesson reminds us of our greatest challenge to becoming like Christ: *self.* When James and John requested positions of authority, Jesus said, "Ye know not what ye ask: can ye drink of the cup that I drink … be baptized with the baptism that I am baptized with?" (Mark 10:38). Jesus was challenging their willingness to share His fate. Scripture indicates that He already knew that they would follow Him in death. They did, indeed, learn the lesson of humble service, as most of the apostles would be martyred for the cause of Christ.

The apostle Paul, in a letter written to one of the churches a couple of decades later, admonishes the believers. "Let this mind be in you, which was also in Christ Jesus: Who, being in the form of God ... made himself of no reputation, and took upon him the form of a servant ... made in the likeness of men... he humbled himself, and became obedient unto death—even the death of the cross!" (Philippians 2:5–8).

Surely the apostles were spiritually impacted by the humility of Jesus that evening. Without a doubt, they never forgot this lesson. Even today the thought of the sovereign Son of God humbly kneeling, washing our feet, stirs our emotions. This illustration from the Master Teacher should be indelibly written in our hearts and minds, because a life of service is not optional. "I have given you an example, that ye should do as I have done to you... The servant is not greater than his lord; neither he that is sent greater than he that sent him. If ye know these things, happy are ye if ye do them" (John 13:15–17).

This is a basic lesson in Christianity. We must learn Jesus's humility, and we must minister to others. May God help us to live this rewarding and pleasant life of humility and service.

Connecting the Dots

- Isaiah 42:1–4
- Isaiah 49:7
- Philippians 2:9–11

Discussions at the Table

Bible Readings: John 13:34, 35; 14:15, 21, 23, 24; 15:1–7, 9–14, 17

The Christian's Identity: Love

How does one recognize a follower of Christ? In John's gospel, Jesus's final exhortation to His apostles at their last supper together, we read at least three requisites that identify the believer.

First, Jesus gave the apostles a "new" commandment. Three times He emphasized, "Love one another" (John 13:34, 15:12, 17). This was not the first time Jesus had instructed His followers to love their fellowman. Who could forget that Jesus taught us to love our enemies and to love our neighbors as ourselves! This "new" commandment to love one another was more specific, however. It was directed to followers of Christ concerning other followers of Christ. Jesus wanted Christians to have fervent love for one another, much like the love in a godly, wholesome family. This love connection with people of like faith would in itself become a testimony of the love of God, identifying us as Christians.

The second identifying requirement was obedience to Christ's teachings. Notably, this requirement is also hinged on love. Jesus was about to be taken from their physical presence. Understanding human nature, we know it was much easier for them to keep His instructions while He was with them. Several times that evening Jesus emphasized that *if they truly loved Him*, they would obey His teaching. Obedience was to be then, and still is today, proof-positive of our love for Jesus. The passion level of our love for Christ can, perhaps, be seen in how fervently we obey.

The final requirement to identity with Christ follows, as a logical consequence or result, the first two—love and obedience. Jesus instructed His followers to "bear fruit." John the Baptist, preparing the way for Jesus's ministry had preached repentance for sin, followed by living a holy life. "Bring forth therefore fruits worthy of repentance," John said (Luke 3:7–9). Giving the analogy that He is a vine and His followers are connecting branches, Jesus explained that for them to remain connected to Him after He left their physical presence, they must be fruitful. This fruitfulness is, in part, a naturally occurring life of virtue that comes about because we love and obey Jesus. Galatians 5 names these virtues, the first of which is, again, love.

Yet there is more to bearing fruit. Jesus taught and trained His followers for a specific purpose: the Great Commission. His disciples were to broadcast, declare, proclaim, and promulgate the gospel, making disciples in all nations, leading others to a saving knowledge of Jesus Christ. They should then disciple and train those who believed to do likewise, just as Jesus had discipled and trained them. When God created man, His first instruction was, "Be fruitful, and multiply, and replenish the earth" (Genesis 1:28). That same command, but in a spiritual concept, is our last instruction from Jesus: "Go ye therefore, and teach all nations, baptizing them... teaching them to observe whatsoever I have commanded you" (Matthew 28:19–20).

Basically, our identity with Christ is based on love (John 3:16). We love Jesus, because He loves us and gave His life for us; so we obey Him, living a virtuous life that exhibits passionate love for others. The fruit of the Spirit (love, joy, peace, patience, kindness, goodness, faithfulness, gentleness, and self-control) endears us to fellow believers and draws sinners to Jesus.

When we think about how the unsaved might be won to Christ, it truly makes sense that love is the key. Love is, appropriately, the greatest human pursuit—the most desired emotion, the most binding attachment, and the most benevolent bias. When nonbelievers witness the true love between and among those in the body of Christ, surely they will be drawn to Christ and His church! What a challenge, then, for members of the Body of Christ to love at the highest level—with a pure heart and fervently (1 Peter 1:22)!

Connecting the Dots

- Jeremiah 31:3
- Psalm 36:5–7
- Deuteronomy 6:5
- Leviticus 19:18

Discussions at the Table

Bible Readings: John 14:12–14; 15:1–2, 7, 16; 16:23; Psalm 77:13–14

Criteria for Answered Prayer

The ministry of Jesus was filled with miracles. Crowds of people sought Him out for their needs and followed Him around, watching in amazement as He healed those who were sick, raised individuals from the dead, cast out demons from those who were tormented and possessed, and more. (See John 20:30; 21:25.) The apostles were present for these miracles, and witnessing Jesus's power confirmed their faith in Him as the Messiah.

Jesus understood, however, that they were still spiritually weak. He knew that once He physically left their presence, the apostles would be shaken. Jesus understood that without the demonstrations of power that fed their faith, their commitment might become feeble. So to build their faith in this last personal exhortation before His death, Jesus assured them that the miracles that validated their faith would not end with His death. Moreover, the miracles would be continued through the apostles themselves. Repeatedly He assured them of God's continuing faithfulness to perform miracles and provide substantiating answers to their requests and needs. Yet this transfer of power was not without prerequisites.

The assurance from John 14:12: "He that believeth on me, the works that I do shall he do also; and greater works than these shall he do." The prerequisite: Have faith in Jesus. Earlier in His ministry the apostles had attempted to cast a demon from a boy but were unsuccessful. When the apostles asked why they were unsuccessful, Jesus replied, "Because of your unbelief. If ye have faith as a grain of mustard seed… nothing shall be impossible unto you" (Matthew 17:14–21).

The assurance from John 14:13–14 says, "Whatsoever ye shall ask in my name… ask anything in my name, I will do it." The prerequisite is to ask (pray to) the Father in Jesus's name. (See John 16:23, 26–27.) This is a very important lesson in how to address our prayers. Our pleas should be directed to God the Father in the name of Jesus. A proper relationship with Jesus gives us the authority to approach the Father with our needs.

The assurance from John 15:7 says, "Ask what ye will, and it shall be done." The prerequisite is to abide (faithfully continue) in Jesus and keep His words alive in your heart. Believe and obey! The Word of God is life and power and judgment. His Word is holy and unchanging. God's character and nature are in His Word. His Word must be ingested and become a part of His followers. (See John 1:1, 14; Hebrews

4:12.) When God's Word is in our hearts, we know how to pray in God's will.

The assurance from John 15:16 says, "Whatsoever ye shall ask of the Father in my name, he may give it you." The prerequisite is to bear fruit. The privilege of this assurance comes only by a rigorous growing process, which is accomplished by living out the holy image of Jesus. We must endure pruning, the work of sanctification. With deliberate resolve, we must stay connected to the Vine, avoiding the decay of worldliness and apathy, which results in severing and discarding. Fruit bearing will then be bountiful, and we will produce fruit that will last (John 15:5–8).

The history of the early Christian church written in the Acts of the Apostles shows how quickly they met the requirements. Surely the boldness that came with the Holy Spirit's infilling escalated the effectiveness of these men.

Connecting the Dots

- Acts 5:12–16
- Mark 11:22–25

Discussions at the Table

Bible Readings: Luke 22:35–37

Understanding the Nature of the Christian Life

"When I sent you without purse, and scrip, and shoes, lacked ye anything?" Jesus asked.

"Nothing," they answered. Earlier in His ministry, Jesus sent the twelve apostles out into the neighboring villages to do God's kingdom work—specifically to preach, drive out demons, and heal the sick. It was a training exercise. At that time Jesus sent them with the instructions not to pack a bag or carry anything with them. They were to take nothing for protection, nothing extra to wear, no food, and no money (Matthew 10, Mark 6, Luke 9). (Later Jesus commissioned seventy others with the same instructions about provisions.) They obeyed, and God provided. When we respond by faith in obedience to God's directives, He always provides.

This time, however, Jesus's instructions were different. This time they should take money, food, necessities, and—a sword! Why had things changed? Why would the peaceable Jesus now tell them they needed a sword? Simply, a war had begun. The advent of Jesus would be the beginning of *spiritual* warfare for His followers that will continue until He returns. Jesus said, "Think not that I am come to send peace on earth: I came not to send peace, but a sword" (Matthew 10:34). Although Jesus lived peaceably on this earth, His righteousness presented an opposing stance to the dominance of sin. It made necessary a choosing of sides—God or Satan; God's Law or man-made rules and regulations; good or evil. So, in this Scripture, Jesus warned His followers *symbolically* that adversity laid ahead.

The psalmist wrote, "Let the high praises of God be in their mouth, and a two-edged sword in their hand" (Psalm 149:6). The apostle Paul would later refer to "armour of righteousness on the right hand and on the left" (2 Corinthians 6:7). In Ephesians 6 Paul described the Christian as a warrior, whose weapon is the sword of the Spirit, which is the Word of God. Paul said, "For though we walk in the flesh, we do not war after the flesh: (For the weapons of our warfare are not carnal, but mighty through God to the pulling down of strong holds;) Casting down imaginations, and every high thing that exalteth itself against the knowledge of God" (2 Corinthians 10:3–5).

A battle laid ahead for Jesus's followers, and so it has been since. "From the days of John the Baptist until now the kingdom of heaven suffereth violence, and the violent take it by force" (Matthew 11:12). They were spiritually strong men, bold men, men with the boldness of the Lion (Revelation 5:5); men with a boldness that comes when we receive the Holy Spirit's empowering! *That boldness* is necessary to commit our lives without reservation to Christ. Satan makes it challenging, but commitment requires determination. *That boldness* is necessary to share our faith. Satan makes us timid, but we must turn the focus away from ourselves and to the needs of others. *That boldness* is necessary to purge evil from society, as much as possible. Satan intimidates us with the muddled legalities of political correctness, but Christians must fearlessly declare righteousness.

At the first event of Jesus sending the apostles out to evangelize, He forewarned them of adversity. To give them perspective on the imminent difficulties they had yet to face, He warned them that they would be ostracized by the religious community, rejected even by family members, persecuted for their belief in Him. "The disciple is not above his master, nor a servant above his lord. It is enough for the disciple that he *be as* his master, and the servant *as* his lord." Jesus reminded His followers that religious leaders opposing Him had accused Him of using Satan's power to do miracles. "If they have called the master of the house Beelzebub (Satan), how much more … them of his household?" (Matthew 10:24–25). This was a forewarning so His followers would not be spiritually shaken when persecution came from the religious elite.

To encourage and comfort them, He said, "Fear not them which kill the body but are not able to kill the soul: but rather, fear him which is able to destroy both soul and body in hell. Fear ye not, therefore, ye are of more value… Whosoever therefore shall confess me before men, him will I confess also before my Father which is in heaven" (Matthcw 10:26–32, select verses).

Living out the Christian life involves daily spiritual warfare, and "we must through much tribulation enter into the kingdom of God" (Acts 14:22). As Christians, we must make every effort to live at peace with everyone (Romans 12:18). Jesus told the apostles in the tumult of His arrest to put away the sword, saying, "All they that take the sword shall perish with the sword" (Matthew 26:52). The Christian's struggle is not against flesh and blood, but it is against powers of darkness and forces of evil (Ephesians 6:10–18). Today, as in Luke 9–10, Jesus sends His disciples again (Acts 1:8). So as good soldiers, we must fight the good fight of faith (1 Timothy 6:12).

Connecting the Dots

- Joshua 1:7–9
- Isaiah 41:10–13

Discussions at the Table

Bible Readings: John 15:18–16:4, 33

Expect Hardship

What the apostles might have thought would be an uneventful meal turned out to be quite different. Jesus assumed the role of a servant and washed their feet, making at least one of them a bit uncomfortable. One from their tight little group was found to be a traitor. The bread and wine of the meal took on deeper meaning, which they surely did not understand. Finally, the news they heard from Jesus was certainly unsettling.

Earlier in Jesus's ministry He spoke about the proper perspective concerning the cost of discipleship.

> If any man come to me, and hate not his father, and mother, and wife, and children, and brethren and sisters, yea, and his own life also, he cannot be my disciple. And whosoever doth not bear his cross, and come after me, cannot be my disciple… whosoever… forsaketh not all that he hath, he cannot be my disciple. (Luke 14:26–33)

More than a warning, this was a touchstone for anyone and everyone, past, present, and future, who would follow Jesus.

A disciple's love for Him must exceed love for all others. The cost of discipleship will be plenary and consuming; so to persevere, heart and mind preparation is required to reach a deliberate resolve.

During the discussions that evening, Jesus forewarned the apostles of being hated by the world and persecuted for their commitment to Him. They could expect to be excommunicated from the synagogue. Even martyrdom might lay ahead for them. According to tradition, with the exception of John, all of the remaining apostles were martyred for Christ. By crucifixion, by sword or spear, by stoning, by hanging, some brutally tortured to death, they joined John the Baptist and Stephen and Paul in martyrdom. Also according to tradition, John was boiled in oil, yet lived. (He was then exiled to the island of Patmos, which God ordained for His divine purpose of recording the Revelation, last book of the Bible.)

Jesus also warned them that evening that He was about to leave them, indicating that they should know the way to where He was going, and that He would return for them. Surely their heads were spinning as Thomas exclaimed, "Lord, we know not whither thou goest; and how can we know the way?" (See John 14:1–5.) Jesus had told them many times that He would be put to death. Interestingly, scripture says that the meaning of this information was hidden from them (Luke 18:34). Perhaps if they had fully comprehended, it would have brought despair. We can see that they did not fully understand all that was about to take place.

Why would Jesus burden His followers with this grim outlook? "These things have I spoken unto you, that ye should not be offended," He said (John 16:1). "These things I have spoken unto you, that in me ye might have peace. In the world ye *shall* have tribulation: but be of good cheer; I have overcome the world" (John 16:33). The knowledge that Jesus knew their future and empathetically warned them would later, when hardship came, become strength and comfort. They, too, would be empowered to "overcome the world."

Connecting the Dots

- Revelation 6:9–11
- Revelation 21:1–4

Discussions at the Table

Bible Readings: John 14:15–18, 26; John 15:26; 16:7–15

Expect the Holy Spirit

Our compassionate Creator understands us—body, soul, and spirit. He knew that walking totally by faith, 100 percent of the time, might possibly, even probably, have been our spiritual demise. To those who experienced Jesus in the flesh, He was reality. His gentle disposition, His deep love and understanding of each individual, His life-changing words, and His amazing miracles were to them spiritual reality. But to those of us who have not experienced Him in the flesh, believing in Jesus the Son of God is (appropriately) an exercise in faith. Perhaps even the apostles might have gradually slipped away from the faith as the powerful memory of Jesus faded from their spirits and difficulty challenged their commitment.

So the Creator sent One who would walk along this spiritual journey with us—One whose personality, like Jesus, is gentle and loving. The constant presence of the Holy Spirit was and is the perfect, wonderful plan for keeping alive the reality of Jesus in our hearts.

Jesus Himself functioned with the aid of the Holy Spirit. We remember that when John baptized Jesus, the Holy Spirit "descended in a bodily shape like a dove" upon Jesus (Luke 3:22). Then Jesus, being *full* of the Spirit, was *led* by the Spirit into the wilderness (Luke 4). With the Spirit's *help*, Jesus endured forty days of fasting and temptation from Satan.

The Christian life still requires faith, which is necessary to please God (Hebrews 11:6). Experiencing the abiding presence of the Holy Spirit, however, moves the Christian life beyond faith to reality—the reality of perceivable companionship and communication, powerful and intimate worship experiences, as well as unprecedented counsel from One who knows all. The Spirit's purposes as counselor to the believer are many. The Holy Spirit is given to teach, bring the words of Jesus to our memory when needed (John 14:26), guide the believer "into all truth," and give revelation of the future (John 16:13). Jesus said the Spirit would empower the believer to share the gospel with unbelievers (Acts 1:8). The benefits of the Holy Spirit's indwelling are immeasurable and completely sufficient.

Jesus said this Counselor would be given to obedient believers. Those who do not accept Jesus cannot receive the Spirit, because they can neither see Him nor perceive His existence (John 14:17). However, the Spirit's purpose among nonbelievers is to help them realize their sin guilt and lovingly draw them to Jesus (John 16:8–11). Thus the

Father *courts* and *woos* sinners to Jesus through the work of the Holy Spirit (John 6:44, 65).

Father, we cannot imagine life without the abiding presence of the Holy Spirit. "Teach me to do thy will, for thou art my God: thy Spirit is good; lead me into the land of uprightness" (Psalm 143:10). We pray in Jesus's name.

Connecting the Dots

- Joel 2:28–29
- Mark 1:4, 7–8
- 1 John 3:24

Discussions at the Table

Bible Reading: Genesis 3; John 6:33–58; Luke 22:14–20

The Living Sacrifice

There were very few rules in the garden of Eden. Fruit from only one forbidden tree in the entire garden was not to be consumed (Genesis 2:16–17). Disobedience to God's rules is sin, and sin cannot be tolerated by the holy and perfect Creator. Sin's penalty is death. "For the wages of sin is death; but the gift of God is eternal life through Christ Jesus our Lord" (Romans 6:23). When Adam and Eve sinned in the garden of Eden, God made garments from animal skin to cover their nudity. We assume this was the first sacrificial death made necessary by sin (Genesis 3:7–10, 21), because "without shedding of blood is no remission (forgiveness)" (Hebrews 9:22). In this early record of humankind lies the first indication of the gravity of sin for humanity and the first shadow of what was yet to come for those who would follow Adam and Eve.

When God delivered the Israelites from Egyptian slavery, the firstborn child and firstborn animals of every household were protected only by the blood of a lamb as the death angel retaliated for Pharaoh's disobedience. "*The blood shall be to you for a token (sign)* upon the houses where ye are: and when

I see the blood, I will pass over you" (Exodus 12:11–13). A sacrifice of life was necessary to preserve life. The scriptures refer to this as the Lord's Passover. From Passover forward, as a continuing ordinance, the ritual of sacrifice was required for the forgiveness of sin.

> The Lord called to Moses, and spake unto him out of the tabernacle of the congregation... "If any man of you bring an offering unto the Lord, ye shall bring your offering of the cattle... herd... flock... without blemish... he shall put his hand upon the head of the burnt offering; and it shall be accepted for him to make atonement for him." (Leviticus 1:1–4)

At the point where the sinner laid his hand upon the head of the animal to be sacrificed, his sin was figuratively transferred to the sacrifice, and the death penalty for sin was suffered by the animal in substitution for the sinner.

"A sign for you," God said. He gave them a sign of His mercy, and that sign was blood. The only way to obtain the blood was by the sacrifice of life—the substitution of one life for another, a lamb for a human being. The blood was and still is an important *sign*. No other substance besides blood is sufficient to take away sin, as sin requires death. Indeed, it was a bloody religion. God received no pleasure, only

propitiation and conciliation, in this method of atonement. But again, it was necessary for sinners to be reconciled to a holy God who could not tolerate sin.

All of the sacrifice and ritual were symbolic, however, of something yet to come. *"A sign for you"* under the Old Covenant foreshadowed the cardinal plan that constituted a New Covenant. In the New Covenant Jesus Himself became the sacrifice for our sins when He shed His blood and died on the cross.

> When [Christ] cometh into the world, he saith… "In burnt offerings and sacrifices for sin thou hast had no pleasure." Then said I, "Lo, I come… to do thy will, O God." He taketh away the first, that he may establish the second… we are sanctified through the offering of the body of Jesus Christ once for all. (From Hebrews 10:5–10; See also Psalm 40:6–8)

At their last supper together that evening, Jesus, soon to become our sacrifice for sin, established a new rite. This liturgy is a way to soberly remember and reflect on His death as our substitute; yet it is also a joyful celebration of our atonement for sin. We are not required to die for our sins, nor must we sacrifice an animal. The sin debt has been paid by the Lamb of God who was "without blemish"—sinless! For those who accept Christ, He has become our Passover Lamb. Hallelujah! How gratefully we celebrate the significance of Holy Communion! "This is my body which is given for you… This cup is the new testament [covenant] in my blood, which is shed for you" (Luke 22:19–20). Precious words!

Lord, our spirits swell with emotion, and our hearts are so grateful! We are eternally glad to be living under the New Covenant. Thank You for taking our punishment for sin. We will certainly always and often remember you with this rite of Holy Communion.

Connecting the Dots

- Hebrews 10:11–14
- Hosea 4:1; 6:6
- Jeremiah 31:31–33; Hebrews 8:8–12
- Isaiah 42:6

Discussions at the Table

Bible Reading: John 14:1–3, 27; 16:16–22, 32

Consolation

On this last evening together, Jesus was brimming with information that He wanted of necessity to convey to His apostles. It was His last chance to show them love, encourage them, instruct them, and warn them before His death. As Jesus prepared to warn them of dreadful events soon to follow, we can hear compassion as He addressed them, "Little children, yet a little while I am with you… whither I go ye cannot come" (John 13:33).

By the end of that evening, they had been told that one of their companions was a betrayer, that Peter would disown Jesus before morning, and that Jesus was leaving. Then, from the heart of Jesus came words that would bring comfort to the apostles. Indeed, these are words renowned that have brought comfort throughout the two thousand years that followed to countless individuals in grief, pain, fear, and despair.

> Let not your heart be troubled: ye believe in God, believe also in me. In my Father's house are many mansions… I go to prepare a place for you. And if I go and prepare a place for you, I

> will come again, and receive you unto myself; that where I am, there ye may be also. (John 14:1–3)

Don't worry. Just trust Me. Surely He had shown Himself powerful and faithful and worthy of trust. "I will pray the Father, and He shall give you another Comforter, that he may abide with you forever; even the Spirit of truth … I will not leave you comfortless" (John 14:16–18). In the hours that followed the apostles would hear many hard warnings, but with each came reassurance.

> If the world hate you, *[yet, keep in mind that]* it hated me before it hated you. (John 15:18)

> A little while, and ye shall not see me: *[yet, then]* a little while and ye shall see me. (John 16:16)

> Ye shall weep and lament, *[yet]* your sorrow shall be turned into joy … ye now therefore have sorrow: *[yet]* I will see you again, and your heart shall rejoice, and your joy no man taketh from you. (John 16:20–22)

Doubtless, much of what Jesus told them was confusing. They did not fully understand it all until after the resurrection. Yet just to hear the Lord's comfort and reassurance was surely soothing. Who else could comfort better than Jesus! He had shown Himself comforting when He calmed the sea and fed the hungry. He had shown Himself consoling when He raised the dead, healed the sick, and cast out demons.

Before they left the upper room that evening, Jesus prayed for them. "Father… they have kept thy Word… They have believed that thou didst send me… I pray for them… I am glorified in them … keep them from the evil… Sanctify them through thy truth; thy Word is truth" (John 17:6–17).

Then Jesus prayed for you and me.

> Neither pray I for these alone, but for them also which shall believe on me through their word; that they all may be one; as thou, Father, art in me, and I in thee, that they also may be one in us: that the world may believe that thou hast sent me. And the glory which thou gavest me I have given them; that they may be one, even as we are one: I in them, and thou in me; that they may be made perfect in one; and that the world may know that thou hast sent me, and hast loved them, as thou hast loved me.
>
> Father, I will that they also, whom thou hast given me, be with me where I am; that they may behold my glory, which thou hast given

me: for thou lovedst me before the foundation of the world. O righteous Father, the world hath not known thee: but I have known thee, and these have known that thou hast sent me. And I have declared unto them thy name, and will declare it: that the love wherewith thou hast loved me may be in them, and I in them. (John 17:20–26)

Part 3

In the Garden

Introduction

The Garden of Gethsemane

When Jesus and the apostles left the upper room following their last meal together, they exited the walled City of Jerusalem. Jerusalem is situated on a spur atop a mountain ridge, so they descended east through the Kidron Valley approaching the slopes of the Mount of Olives. They were en route to a place called Gethsemane, where olive trees grew in abundance. It was surely a peaceful place, perhaps a garden-like setting, where they frequently met together.

As they made their way to Gethsemane, Jesus continued to warn and instruct them. With His suffering drawing near, Matthew's gospel records that Jesus was sorrowful and troubled in His spirit. The apostles recognized His anguish; perhaps His conversation seemed foreboding with the dread He carried. Obviously the omniscient Lord knew His ordeal would begin in Gethsemane.

There are lessons to be learned in the garden.

In the Garden

Bible Reading: Mark 14:26–31

Reverent Dependency on God

When Jesus and the apostles concluded their meal, they left the upper room and went toward the Mount of Olives. It is not clear from scripture whether this conversation took place in the upper room or as they walked to the Garden of Gethsemane. Matthew's and Mark's gospels indicate that perhaps on their way to the garden, Jesus continued to warn the apostles of what to expect. "All ye shall be offended [caused to stumble] because of me this night," He foretold.

Peter responded that even if all the rest of the apostles were caused to stumble or take offense, he would not. Peter loved Jesus; he had noble and sincere intentions, but he had a tendency to be brash and adamant. The omniscient and loving Lord knew Peter's weaknesses and his future. Jesus knew that within that same twenty-four hours, Peter would go from gallant defender with a sword (Mark 14:47) to wavering, cursing coward (Mark 14:67–71). We can learn from Peter's mistakes.

When we become comfortable in any relationship, speaking without thinking can become a snare. When we commune with the Almighty, however, we should guard our words.

The writer of Ecclesiastes 5:2 warned, "Be not rash with thy mouth, and let not thine heart be hasty to utter any thing before God … therefore let thy words be few." Jesus gave similar instruction on how to pray. "When ye pray, use not vain repetitions, as the heathen do: for they think that they shall be heard for their much speaking … your Father knoweth what things ye have need of, before ye ask him" (Matthew 6:7–8). Yet, in our prayers, have we attempted to be manipulative? Have we tried to blame, whine, or bargain with God? Have we made rash promises to Him? Have we lost reverent awareness of His holiness and power and omniscience?

God's constant presence and His intimate nature allow us to be comfortable with Him. But take caution! In that same comfortable intimacy of relationship with the Almighty, it is possible that we might neglect to *revere* Him. God sees and knows each of us thoroughly. He knows our strengths and weaknesses, as well as what lies ahead in our future. He knows the words of our mouths before they are ever conceived in our minds (Psalm 139:4)! How amazing is His power and knowledge and wisdom! More amazing still are His mercy and grace and love toward us.

Perhaps our earthly conversations should reflect humility and dependency on God. Perhaps our declarations and intentions should be seasoned with phrases such as "by the grace of God" and "if the Lord is willing" (James 4:13–17). If in all our ways we acknowledge the Lord, then we can expect His direction and help (Proverbs 3:6). Perhaps our intentions and vows to God should be made with solemnity, having spent considerable time in thought before speaking. Perhaps our prayer should be for God to open our spiritual eyes to perceive more of His holiness and power, so that we might revere Him more—to perceive more of His mercy and grace, so that we might love Him more.

Connecting the Dots

- Psalm 103:8–18

In the Garden

Bible Reading: Matthew 26:36–45; Luke 22:39–45

Agonizing Alone

In the Garden of Gethsemane, Jesus asked the apostles to sit and wait at a certain point, saying to them, "Sit ye here, while I go and pray yonder." He took with Him Peter, and brothers James and John, further into the garden. He said to the three men, "My soul is exceeding sorrowful, even unto death: tarry ye here, and watch with me." Jesus knew the severity of the trials and temptations that lay minutes ahead for His followers. He had warned them earlier that evening of a betrayal, a denial, and division in their close-knit group. He had also warned repeatedly of His impending death. He knew how close was the upheaval among His followers and how near was the end of His earthly ministry.

"Rise and pray, lest ye enter into temptation," He instructed. Then, moving about a stone's throw away from them, Jesus, feeling overwhelmed with sorrow and dread, fell with His face to the ground and began an agonizing prayer to His Father. Twice He pleaded with God, "Father, if it be possible let this cup pass from me," always adding, "Thy will be done." Imagine the dread! Not only did He foreknow the extent of His physical suffering, but He would also soon assume the weight of the sins of the whole world, past and future. (Anyone who has realized and internally carried guilt for a sin they committed knows the weight upon one's spirit.) "And being in agony, he prayed more earnestly: and his sweat was as it were drops of blood falling down to the ground!" Surely never before or since has anyone prayed with such passion as Jesus did that night. We can identify with His humanity and empathize to some extent; yet *no one else* has ever carried this emotional and spiritual weight. Surely the heart of the Father was saddened by the agony of His Son! An angel came to Jesus and strengthened Him.

In the garden the apostles could sense that Jesus was anguished. They knew of imminent peril and sensed the urgency with which He asked them to watch and pray. Yet the apostles, "exhausted from sorrow" after hearing distressing news at supper, were found sleeping. It was late; they were tired and emotionally exhausted. Praying, then, became difficult, and sleep was anxiety's relief. Consequently, they were unprepared for the difficult times ahead. Jesus, upon finding them asleep, said, "Could ye not watch with me one hour? … the spirit is willing, but the flesh is weak."

Jesus knows and understands the weakness of our human frames, yet the challenge remains our own. The struggle to discipline ourselves to pray lies within the individual's will. The Holy Spirit is ready to empower us, yet that initial effort must be made by our flesh.

Many of the same dangers faced by the apostles threaten Christians today. Jesus urged His followers repeatedly to face the difficulties and the commonplace with prayer. Pray for your enemies; pray to escape temptation; pray to escape the wrath of God in judgment; pray for one another; pray without ceasing; watch and pray. Peter, overwhelmed and sleepy on the night of Jesus's arrest, later learned the lesson. He wrote, "The end of all things is at hand: be ye therefore sober, and watch unto prayer" (1 Peter 4:7).

This is a command to all of us today: Discipline your mind and body, and pray. Satan actively works to hinder our prayer life with distractions, fatigue, and busyness; so we must be aggressive, offensive, and defensive in our prayer efforts. When we understand the absolute necessity of prayer, we realize it is important to plan ahead, set a time and place, make it happen. We must be victorious in this battle! Prayer is our lifeline! Prayer is our victory—for effectiveness and, ultimately, winning the spiritual war.

O soul, be still and listen. Is Jesus calling us to commune with Him? Does He bid us spend one hour in His presence?

Connecting the Dots

- Matthew 6:6, 9–13

In the Garden

Bible Reading: Luke 22:1–6; John 13:18–30; Matthew 26:14, 15; 27:3–10

Judas and the Betrayal

Early in Jesus's ministry He chose from His disciples twelve men, whom He designated apostles, to be a select group. The omniscient Lord was not misguided when He chose Judas Iscariot to be one of the twelve apostles. He selected these men after having prayed all night (Luke 6:12–16). Quoting from Psalm 41:9, Jesus applied the words prophetically to His betrayal. "I speak not of you all: I know whom I have chosen: but that the scripture may be fulfilled, 'He that eateth bread with me hath lifted up his heel against me'" (John 13:18).

Judas had probably seen Jesus calm a storm on the Sea of Galilee and walk on water. He had probably witnessed Jesus's raising the dead and healing the sick. Judas had eaten from the loaves and fish miraculously increased by Jesus. Judas was even among the Twelve who were given power and authority to drive out demons, heal the sick, and preach the gospel in various villages (Mark 6; Luke 9)! It is inconceivable that one could walk daily with Jesus, experience His passion and purity, witness His miracles, and hear His wise teaching, and not be spiritually elevated to commitment. Yet Luke's gospel records, "Satan [entered] Judas, surnamed Iscariot, being [one of] the twelve" (Luke 22:3). Judas's soul must have been acquiescent to Satan; certainly he appears to have had sinful inclinations, as John characterized Judas as a "thief" (John 12:4–6). So, considering that Judas was being paid to betray, we might assume that his love of money was perhaps his downfall.

Prior to their last supper together, when first "Satan entered Judas" concerning betrayal for profit, he approached the chief priests and agreed to arrange an occasion to hand over Jesus in exchange for money. He received thirty silver shekels, the price of a slave. Then on the evening before Passover, Judas duplicitously joined with Jesus and the other apostles to take part in an evening meal. During the course of that intimate time together, Jesus washed Judas's feet. One wonders what thoughts went through the mind of Christ as He washed the feet of the one He knew had conspired to betray Him already. Surely His emotions were building, as John records that Jesus was *troubled in spirit*. When Jesus exposed Judas as the betrayer that evening, Judas, with no obvious remorse, promptly moved forward with his plan. As soon as Judas took the bread, "Satan entered into him" (again), and Judas "went immediately out: and it was night" (John 13:27, 30).

Jesus and the apostles, having left the room where they had shared that evening meal, crossed the Kidron Valley. He and the apostles went into the garden there. "Judas also … knew the place: for Jesus ofttimes resorted thither with his disciples" (John 18:1–2). As Jesus finished preparing Himself through prayer for His imminent torture and death, Judas arrived with a crowd of soldiers armed with swords and clubs. Judas had arranged a signal with the authorities. "Whomsoever I shall kiss, that same is he; take him, and lead him away safely." Judas went directly to Jesus and said, "'Master;'… and kissed him" (Mark 14:44–45).

We can try to imagine how Jesus might have felt in this situation. Human reaction for most of us might have been to wince when an enemy/traitor gets in your face. Did Jesus's heart race or His face flush as He controlled the complicated emotions of the moment? Jesus does not appear disquieted, although perhaps He felt violated. Doubtless He felt the pain of betrayal by one He called "friend."

> Lord, help us to examine our lives for sins of betrayal. Have we been disloyal in failing to witness? Have we been unfaithful in fulfilling our vows to You? Have we disappointed the hopes and expectations You have for us? Have we denied knowing You by failing to represent

You in public ways? Have we, like the apostles that evening, neglected to pray? "Search me, O God, and know my heart: try me, and know my thoughts. See if there be any wicked way in me, and lead me in the way everlasting" (Psalm 139:23–24).

Connecting the Dots

- Zechariah 11:10–13
- Psalm 41:9

In the Garden

Bible Reading: Matthew 26:47–56; Mark 14:43–50; Luke 22:47–53; John 18:2–11

The Arrest of Jesus

Darkness is often the time when evil men practice their evil deeds, as if the darkness would cover their sins. We are not surprised that Judas waited for the cover of darkness, nor are we surprised that the chief priests and elders looked for a clandestine way to arrest Jesus. So among the stealthy crowd who came in the cover of darkness to arrest Him were Judas, officials sent by the chief priests and elders, and a detachment of soldiers.

> Jesus, therefore, knowing all things that should come upon him, went forth, and said unto them, "Whom seek ye?" They answered him, "Jesus of Nazareth." Jesus saith unto them, "I am he." (John 18:4–5)

An interesting thing happened in this encounter that is only recorded in John's gospel. When Jesus said, "I am He," the arresting crowd drew back and fell to the ground! We can only speculate about what prompted this response. Perhaps it was because Jesus was forthright and open, when the soldiers expected to find someone running to escape arrest. Maybe it was His gentleness and humility, when they were expecting a criminal personality. (Possibly, when the Creator of the Universe spoke His name, "I AM," there was explosive power such as gives impetus, driving the group to the ground!)

Although Jesus had dealt openly and peaceably with the local religious leaders, His authoritative responses to their verbal challenges were a source of antagonism to them. Verbally, Jesus did not mince words in His discussions with the Pharisees on how they had distorted God's laws. Daily Jesus had taught at the temple and healed the sick. The chief priests and teachers of the law were often present. They heard the same words and saw the same miracles that drew others to Jesus, but their hearts were full of unrighteousness. Simply stated, Jesus's convicting words reached the core of their sin and exposed their unrighteousness. Instead of responding to guilt with repentance, wickedness began to grow in their hearts, building to revenge. This is Satan's way. Thus, in the cover of darkness came this cowardly entourage, carrying swords and clubs, to arrest a man whose *only* weapon had been His poignant words.

Jesus's ministry on this earth was peaceable, teaching and showing love and kindness. He was human, however, so surely He could be riled. Yet His passions that could be stirred were not selfish issues, but issues of unrighteousness and injustice. Possibly the most intense demonstration of His earthly life was to drive irreverent and dishonest merchants from the sacred temple. All four gospels portray Jesus as gentle, compassionate, attending the needs of people, drawn to children and those most desperate. Jesus did not mince words when defining sin, but He was not an agitator or rabble-rouser. He taught, "Blessed are the peacemakers" (Matthew 5:9). He taught that for us to be seasoned Christians, we should live at peace with one another (Mark 9:50).

What an anomaly, then, that Jesus would be arrested by a large crowd armed with swords and clubs! Jesus reasoned with the crowd (whom He appeared to recognize) who came to arrest Him. "Are ye come out as against a thief with swords and staves for to take me? I sat daily with you teaching in the temple, and ye laid no hold on me" (Matthew 26:55).

As the soldiers seized and arrested Jesus, there was confusion and fear among the apostles, and then a skirmish between the apostles and the authorities. When the apostles saw what was about to happen, they said, "Lord, shall we smite with the sword?" (Luke 22:49). Not waiting for an answer, "Simon Peter having a sword drew it, and smote the high priest's servant (Malchus), and cutting off his right ear" (John 18:10). Peter was known to be impetuous in his actions and words.

Surely Peter had spent enough time with Jesus to know His power to do miracles; yet in his haste and fervor, he tried to take matters into his own hands. How painfully we might identify with Peter! The sinful man in us would return blow for blow.

Jesus touched the man's ear and healed him (Luke 22:51). Jesus instructed, "Put up again thy sword into his place: for all they that take the sword shall perish with the sword. Thinkest thou that I cannot now pray to my Father, and he shall presently give me more than twelve legions of angels?" (Matthew 26:52–53). (One wonders if, when those words were spoken, all in heaven stood thunderously to their feet, at attention and in readiness, like a great army eagerly awaiting the command to rescue their Beloved!) "Then all the disciples forsook him, and fled" (Matthew 26:56).

In those chaotic and tense moments, Jesus, the Son of Man, maintained composure and remained sinless. Jesus, the Master Teacher, demonstrated four ways to gently deal with our enemies. First, when confronted by Judas as betrayer, Jesus addressed him kindly as "friend." Then Jesus showed compassion for the physical state of Malchus, healing his severed ear. Further, when Peter, though well-meaning, would have deterred Him from the divine plan of God, Jesus reasoned with him using scripture. (See Genesis 9:6.) Finally,

Jesus had found strength from God through prayer, for who is better able to help than He who commands legions of angels!

Connecting the Dots

- Zechariah 13:7

Part 4

The Suffering of Christ

Introduction

Lest We Forget

No person, no race or nation of people, and no human authority took the life of Jesus. It was the sins of all humankind, individually and collectively, past and future, that required and constrained His willing sacrifice.

> Therefore doth my Father love me, because I lay down my life, that I might take it again. No man taketh it from me, but I lay it down of myself. I have power to lay it down, and I have power to take it again. (John 10:17–18)

He knew well ahead the horrific death He would die. He was human, and He felt dread.

> My soul is exceeding sorrowful, even unto death… He… fell on his face, and prayed, saying, "O my Father, if it be possible, let this cup pass from me: nevertheless not as I will, but as thou wilt." (Matthew 26:38–39)

He had the option to prevent it.

> Thinkest thou that I cannot now pray to my Father, and he shall presently give me more than twelve legions of angels? But how then shall the scriptures be fulfilled, that thus it must be? (Matthew 26:53–54)

So He lovingly and faithfully chose to make the greatest sacrifice.

> Therefore we ought to give the more earnest heed to the things which we have heard, lest at any time we should let them slip. For if the word spoken by angels was stedfast, and every transgression and disobedience received a just recompence of reward; how shall we escape, if we neglect so great salvation? (Hebrews 2:1–3a)

Though words cannot fully describe the pain, anguish, and humiliation Jesus endured, let us walk through His suffering, lest we forget.

The Suffering of Christ

Bible Reading: Matthew 26:57–68

Jesus before the Sanhedrin

The priesthood and religious leadership had become corrupt. The spiritual leaders of the Jewish people had become power hungry and controlling, adding their own personal rules and regulations to the Law given by God through Moses, thereby making life more burdensome for the laity. The priests had come to enjoy the power and status of religious elites and wanted deference, obeisance, privilege, and veneration. This was very much troubling to Jesus, who was the fulfillment of the Law, having come to *lift* the burdens of the people and to fulfill and accomplish the consummate plan.

Though the priesthood knew the prophecies of the Messiah, Jesus was not what they expected or wanted as their Messiah. Scripture indicates that Jesus was not the regal, handsome figure that commanded obedience and admiration, but rather, was humble and gentle. Perhaps, in their carnal opinions, they were hoping for a Messiah who would validate and join them in their pursuits for power. Whatever the motivation, the Jewish authorities in opposition to Jesus did not want to believe that Jesus was sent from God.

At one earlier confrontation with the Pharisees, Jesus testified to being the Son of God. "I am one that bear witness of myself, and the Father that sent me beareth witness of me" (John 8:18 with Deuteronomy 17:6). "I proceeded forth and came from God; neither came I of myself, but he sent me" (John 8:42). The challenge continued, to which Jesus responded, revealing His eternal nature and echoing the same declaration of identity spoken millennia earlier (Exodus 3:14). "Verily, verily I say unto you, before Abraham was, I AM!" (John 8:58).

John 12 gives the frustrating account of their disbelief. "But though he had done so many miracles before them, yet they believed not on him: That the saying of [Isaiah] the prophet might be fulfilled, which he spake" (John 12:37–38; See Isaiah 6:10; also 53:1). At their last supper together, Jesus, helping His apostles to understand the battle ahead, said, "If I had not come and spoken unto them … If I had not done among them the works which none other man did, they had not had sin: but now they have both seen and hated both me and my Father. But this cometh to pass, that the word might be fulfilled that is written … they hated me without a cause" (John 15:24–25; see also Psalm 35:19; 69:4).

On the evening Jesus was arrested, the chief priests conducted a mock trial during the night. (It was considered unlawful for the Sanhedrin to convene at night.) It was an opportunity for them to vent their anger, as Jesus was blindfolded, struck with fists, and slapped. They scoffed, derided Him, and spat in the face of the Son of God. At the mock trial by the Sanhedrin, supreme council for the Jewish people, on the evening before His death, the high priest demanded to know: "I adjure thee by the living God: … Tell us whether thou be the Christ, the Son of God." Jesus affirmed that He is, and replied, "Hereafter shall ye see the Son of man sitting on the right hand of power, and coming in the clouds of heaven" (Matthew 26:63–64).

Another "legal" session was called early the next morning at which the decision was made to put Jesus to death. The high priest considered Jesus's claim to be the Christ to be blasphemous, and the Sanhedrin declared, "He is guilty of death." Because of His claim to be the Son of God, they declared Him *worthy* of death. Oh, the irony of that verdict! As the sinless Son of Man and Son of God, He was the only One who qualified as *worthy*—the only sinless One whose death could atone for our sins. He completed the task of fulfilling the Law with a victorious, "It is finished" (John 19:30). In eternity we will join the angels declaring, "Worthy is the Lamb that was slain to receive power, and riches, and wisdom, and strength, and honour, and glory, and blessing!" (Revelation 5:12).

Connecting the Dots

- Psalm 110:1
- Revelation 5
- Isaiah 53:2–3

The Suffering of Christ

Bible Reading: Matthew 26:57–68; 27:11–31; Luke 23:1, 2

Mockery and Torture

Isaiah had prophesied concerning the Suffering Servant (52–53) that He would not be a handsome, imposing persona. Further, His life would be fraught with rejection, sorrow, and suffering. When Jesus began His public ministry, opinions of Him became polarized. He was loved by His closest associates, but those in religious authority opposed Him. Jesus experienced disloyalty—the loss of friends and disciples (John 6:41–66). There are indications that His biological half-brothers did not believe in Him until later in His life (John 7:5). John wrote of the sad plight of Jesus: "He was in the world, and the world was made by him, and the world knew him not. He came unto his own, and his own received him not" (John 1:10–11). Jesus was surely harassed by Satan. Scripture says of Jesus that He was "in all points tempted like we are, yet [was] without sin" (Hebrews 4:15). As the end of His earthly life drew near, Jesus had spoken to comfort and encourage His apostles. "If the world hate you, ye know that it hated me before it hated you" (John 15:18).

We remember that less than a week before His death, Jesus had returned to Jerusalem with fanfare (Matthew 21).

The chief priests, Pharisees, and Sadducees, however, had challenged Him those last few days with questions designed to snare, as they looked for a way to arrest Him. In a final warning directed at the teachers of the law and Pharisees, Jesus defined their sins with seven condemning "woes." "Ye serpents, ye generation of vipers, how can ye escape the damnation of hell?" He exclaimed (Matthew 23). They were so angered that the meeting was held to plot Jesus's arrest and death. Judas Iscariot had provided a clandestine opportunity to seize and arrest Jesus. Jesus was taken before Pilate by the religious authorities and accused of attempting to subvert the Jewish nation, perverting the people, and thereby, undermining the religious authorities (Luke 23:2, 13–14).

Pilate ordered that Jesus be scourged. Roman whips, made on the order of the cat-o-nine-tails, were lethal. The whips had multiple straps that were laced with pieces of glass and metal. Many a victim did not survive a flogging of this kind. Most of the flesh from Jesus's torso would have been mutilated, perhaps even removed, by this instrument of death. "His visage was so marred more than any man, and his form more than the sons of men" (Isaiah 52:13–15).

While Jesus awaited crucifixion, the soldiers were without compassion for His mutilated condition. They stripped

Him of His clothes and put another robe on His tender, bleeding body for the purpose of mocking Him. One can only imagine how cruelly these brutal soldiers placed on His head a crown made of thorns. Then a staff they intended as a mock scepter was used to strike His precious head again and again. Unrelenting, they beat Him with their fists as well.

As we recount the sufferings of Jesus, we must remember that His presence on earth was for the purpose of redeeming *us*. Therefore, it seems appropriate to study and contemplate His suffering by conscious self-subjection—imagining ourselves enduring the abuse, because His experience was in our stead and on our behalf. When we meditate upon the ghastly and appalling suffering of Jesus for us, we feel constrained to thank Him. If we lift our voices to thank Him even now, perhaps the eternal Son of God, unconfined by time, could hear as He was being tortured and dying in our stead. Perhaps our gratitude will have helped Him endure. Thank You, Jesus!

Connecting the Dots

- Isaiah 53
- Isaiah 50:4–9
- Hebrews 2:9, 10

The Suffering of Christ

Bible Reading: Matthew 27:32–61; Mark 15:21–47; Luke 23:26–55; John 19:16–42

Crucifixion

Pilate relinquished Jesus to the soldiers to be crucified, as the crowd of onlookers shouted, "Crucify Him!" Crucifixion was a death sentence, but it was designed to bring about a slow and excruciating demise. It was also a punishment designed to humiliate—publicity, nakedness, and the curse associated with death by hanging on a tree. "Christ hath redeemed (sinners) from the curse of the law, being made a curse for us: for it is written; 'Cursed is everyone that hangeth on a tree'" (Deuteronomy 21:22–23; Galatians 3:13).

Under the charge of the governor's soldiers, Jesus left the court setting, a place called the Stone Pavement. According to John's gospel, Jesus started out carrying His own cross. One can imagine that He was not able to carry it far, considering the wounds from the scourging. A man named Simon, who was passing by at the time, was forced to carry the cross for Jesus. The entourage with Jesus (which included His followers, soldiers, and two criminals, also to be crucified) proceeded outside of the walled city to a place called Golgotha. It was there, outside the city gate (Hebrews 13:11–12), that Jesus was crucified.

Jesus was offered a pain-killing narcotic mixed with wine, which He tasted and then refused (Matthew 26:29). Around nine o'clock in the morning, the soldiers crucified Him, driving spikes into His hands and into His feet. Jesus their Creator knew those soldiers. He knew that they did not understand the heinous atrocity they were committing, and He pleaded their innocence before the Father. "Father, forgive them; for they know not what they do" (Luke 23:34).

Soldiers guarding the cross, in the presence of Jesus and without sensitivity, divided up Jesus's clothing between them and then cast lots (gambled) for His (probably more valuable) garment. "They part my garments among them, and cast lots upon my vesture" (Psalm 22:18).

All of the physical and emotional pain, sickness and weakness that humans suffer, Jesus took upon Himself as He hung on the cross. All of our sins over the course of a lifetime—intentional sins, sins of omission, especially those greatest regrets that left us with heavy guilt and remorse—were placed upon Jesus. All of the sins of every individual, past and future—sins of the whole world—were placed upon Jesus! We cannot imagine the crushing, piercing weight He felt.

> Surely he hath borne our griefs, and carried our sorrows: yet we did esteem him stricken, smitten of God, and afflicted. But he was wounded for *our* transgressions, he was bruised for *our* iniquities: the chastisement of *our* peace was upon him; and with his stripes we are healed. All we like sheep have gone astray; we have turned every one to his own way; and the Lord hath laid on him the iniquity of us all. (Isaiah 53:4–6)

As He struggled to breathe and writhed in pain, the chief priests, the teachers of the Law and the elders mocked Jesus. The criminals who were crucified on either side of Jesus also taunted Him. "But I am a worm and no man; a reproach of men, and despised of the people. All they that see me laugh me to scorn: they shoot out the lip, they shake the head, saying, 'He trusted on the Lord that he would deliver him: let him deliver him, seeing he delighted in him'" (Psalm 22:6–8; Matthew 27:41–44).

Then Luke's gospel indicates that one of those crucified with Jesus began to experience compassion and quite possibly, conviction for sin. The criminal, drawn to Jesus and realizing his own eternal nature, asked to be remembered by Jesus in the future or afterlife. There, at the cross, the first person was forgiven after the shedding of Jesus's blood—the first soul to be washed in the blood of the Lamb of God! How marvelous! Thus salvation began, as Jesus replied, "Verily I say unto thee, Today shalt thou be with me in paradise" (Luke 23:43).

Around noon the sun ceased shining, and the whole land became dark.

> "It shall come to pass in that day," saith the Lord God, "that I will cause the sun to go down at noon, and I will darken the earth in the clear day: I will turn your feasts into mourning, and all your songs into lamentation. I will bring up sackcloth upon all loins, and baldness upon every head… I will make it as the mourning of an only son, and the end thereof as a bitter day." (Amos 8:9–10)

For another three agonizing hours Jesus suffered.

> "I am poured out like water, and all my bones are out of joint. My heart is like wax; it has melted in the midst of my bowels. My strength is dried up like a potsherd; and my tongue cleaveth to my jaws; and thou hast brought me into the dust of death. Dogs have compassed

> me; the assembly of the wicked have enclosed me: they pierced my hands and my feet … they look and stare upon me." (Psalm 22:14–17)

Around three o'clock in the afternoon, Jesus cried out with a loud voice, "My God, my God, why hast thou forsaken me?" (Psalm 22:1). Surely the weight of the sins of the world, my sin, had been placed upon His dying body and His spirit. "For hc hath made him to be sin for us, who knew no sin; that we might be made the righteousness of God in him" (2 Corinthians 5:21). Only a few hours earlier He explained, "I came from the Father, and am come into the world: again, I leave the world, and go to the Father" (John 16:28). He cried aloud, "Father, into thy hands I commend my spirit" (Psalm 31:5). The omnipotent Son of God declared, "It is finished: and he bowed his head, and gave up the ghost" (John 19:30). Jesus, our Paschal Lamb, was crucified and died on the day and approximate time that all in Israel were sacrificing the Passover lambs.

The darkness continued. At His death an earthquake occurred, and the veil in the temple that cordoned the Holy of Holies was torn in half, top to bottom. Symbolically and literally, direct access to the presence of God was available to everyone who would come in the name of Jesus, our High Priest. When the centurion and those guarding the cross "saw the earthquake, and those things that were done, they feared greatly, saying, 'Truly this was the Son of God!'" (Matthew 27:54). (See also Mark 15:39, Luke 23:47.)

The bodies of the three who were crucified had to be removed quickly, as Passover began at evening (around six o'clock). To hasten the death of those crucified, their legs were broken. However, when the soldiers came to Jesus, they saw that He was already dead and did not break His legs (Exodus 12:46–47). Instead, one of the soldiers pierced Jesus's side with a spear, from which there was a sudden flow of blood and water.

> "And I will pour out upon the house of David, and upon the inhabitants of Jerusalem, the spirit of grace and of supplications: and they shall look upon me whom they have pierced, and they shall mourn for him, as one mourneth for his only son, and shall be in bitterness for him, as... for his first-born son. In that day there shall be a fountain opened to the house of David and to the inhabitants of Jerusalem for sin and for uncleanness." (Zechariah 12:10; 13:1)

> "Yet it pleased the Lord to bruise him; he hath put him to grief: when thou shalt make his soul an offering for sin, he shall see his seed, he shall

prolong his days, and the pleasure of the Lord shall prosper in his hand." (Isaiah 53:10)

Connecting the Dots

- Psalm 22 (See also Zechariah 12:10–13:1)
- Leviticus 5
- Philippians 2:5–11
- Acts 4:12
- Revelation 5:6–13

Part 5

Between Death and Resurrection

Bible Reading: Matthew 27:62–66

Adversity

God allows difficulty in our lives to transform His children to the image of Jesus. It is in the difficulties that we gain spiritual strength, learn to trust God, develop character, and learn of life.

> We glory in tribulations... knowing that tribulation [produces] patience; And patience [produces] experience; and experience [produces] hope: And hope maketh not ashamed; because the love of God is shed abroad in our hearts by the Holy Ghost, which is given unto us. (Romans 5:2–5)

It is also in the difficulties that we feel closest to God; further, difficulties help us realize our need of God. "The Lord is nigh unto them that are of a broken heart; and saveth such as be of a contrite spirit" (Psalm 34:18).

During the time between Jesus's arrest and His resurrection, His followers experienced spiritual and emotional turmoil. They were *frightened* to the point of desertion on the evening of Jesus's arrest. John and perhaps one other apostle must have then followed close by to witness Jesus's trial. The two were allowed into the high priest's courtyard. Peter, however, remained outside the courtyard, fearing to be identified with Jesus. Realizing Peter's fear of identity reveals the *danger* he felt because of his association with Jesus (Matthew 26:69–75).

The crucifixion was a public event. Luke 23:49 records, "All his acquaintance, and the women that followed him from Galilee, stood afar off, beholding these things." Watching the horrific death of their friend was surely *distressing.* Perhaps, having seen His power displayed in numerous miraculous ways, they expected Jesus to miraculously save Himself. If so, they were *disappointed.* The apostles had mistakenly expected Jesus to deliver Israel from Roman rule and set up His kingdom, but their leader was now dead, and they were surely *disillusioned.*

The chief priests were suspicious of Jesus's followers, expecting them to attempt to steal His body. So the apostles probably felt they were *under official scrutiny.* They probably feared repercussions for themselves in the days to come, because surely they remembered Jesus had warned of persecution over their last meal together. As comrades they remained together the following Sunday, *mourning the loss* of their leader and their hopes. John's gospel records that the apostles were fearfully huddling together behind locked doors *dreading* what might be their own fate (John 20:19).

Jesus knew their lives would be difficult. He warned them and encouraged them at their last meal together. "These things have I told you, that when the time shall come, ye may remember that I told you of them" (John 16:4). "These things I have spoken unto you, that in me ye might have peace. In the world ye shall have tribulation: But be of good cheer" (John 16:33).

Indeed, life for Jesus's followers was very difficult—but it was necessary. You see, there was a divine plan. It was a plan that was well thought out and perfected, designed before time began (Revelation 13:8b). It was a plan revealed many years in advance, foretold by prophets, documented and anticipated. It was a plan with many purposes, because our needs were many—revelation, redemption, teaching, healing. It was a plan completed in the fullness of time. Every detail was actualized with perfection, all with the greatest of love for humankind, collectively and individually. None of it was happenstance.

With the same providential power, God still directs His plans, the one for you and the one for me, with all of them working together individually and collectively. "A man's heart deviseth his way: but the Lord directeth his steps" (Proverbs 16:9). "Man's goings are of the Lord; how can a man then understand his own way?" (Proverbs 20:24). So do not become anguished as the plan for you becomes complicated in your understanding. And do not become dismayed when the plan for you takes you through difficulty. Nothing He plans is happenchance, and He is never without sovereign control. "For I know the thoughts that I think toward you, saith the Lord, thoughts of peace, and not of evil, to give you an expected end" (Jeremiah 29:11). When we belong to Him, there is for each of us a divine plan—the very best plan for us. When your plan is completed by Him, you will stroll leisurely with Him and be soothed in eternity. As an old song once assured us, "We will understand it better bye and bye."[1]

> Jesus lifted up his eyes to heaven and said, "Father, the hour is come; glorify thy Son, that thy Son also may glorify thee … I have manifested thy name unto the men which thou gavest me out of the world … I pray for them … Holy Father, keep through thine own name those whom thou hast given me, that they may be one, as we are … these things I speak in the world, that they might have my joy fulfilled in themselves … I pray not that thou shouldest take them out of the world, but that thou shouldest keep them from the evil … Neither pray I for these alone, but for them also which shall believe on me through their word." (John 17, select verses)

---

[1] "We'll Understand It Better By and By," Charles Albert Tindley (Public Domain)

Part 6

The Reality of Resurrection

Introduction

Reality Defined

The word *reality* is defined as follows: (Philosophy) "Existence that is absolute, self-sufficient, or objective, and not subject to human decisions or conventions." [2]

God is "I AM," the absolute reality of the universe, existing independently and self-sufficiently. He is the source from which all other things derive. By and at His will, "were all things created, that are in heaven, and that are in earth, visible and invisible ... all things were created by him and for him ... he is before all things and by him all things consist" (Colossians 1:16–17).

Consider this: At God's will all other things could conceivably cease to be reality, yet He would remain. This will never happen, however, because of one fundamental axiom: "God is not a man, that he should lie; neither the son of man, that

[2] Author: OxfordDictionaries.com Publisher: Oxford University Press Date: [2019] Author: OxfordDictionaries.com Publisher: Oxford University Press Date: [2019].

he should repent [change his mind]" (Numbers 23:19). God had a divine plan, and He had made a promise: redemption. That scripture continues: "Hath he said, and shall he not do it? Or hath he spoken, and shall he not make it good?" The immutable Sovereign never makes a mistake, nor does He, in His absolute perfection, change His course. This attribute is a great comfort for humanity.

The reality of His word in Scripture is seen in the proof: He promised redemption, and redemption has been provided. The resurrected Redeemer is proof and reality. "He was buried … rose again the third day according to the scriptures… he was seen of above five hundred brethren at once" (1 Corinthians 15:4–6). After his suffering, "he shewed himself alive … by many infallible proofs, being seen of them forty days, and speaking of the things pertaining to the kingdom of God" (Acts 1:3).

The four gospels reveal eleven specific events where Jesus appeared personally to individuals and groups after His resurrection. Let us look at some of those specific events.

The Reality of Resurrection

Bible Reading: Luke 23:50–24:11

Burial and Resurrection—the First to Know

Preparation for Jesus's burial had actually begun six days before Jesus was crucified. We remember that when Jesus was having dinner at the home of Simon in the town of Bethany, Mary anointed Jesus with the jar of expensive perfume (spikenard), which she poured (possibly) on both His head and feet (John 11:2). Jesus defended her generous act of love and worship, saying, "She did it for my burial" (Matthew 26:10, 12; also Mark 14, John 12).

Isaiah 53:9 prophesied, "He made his grave with the wicked, and with the rich in his death; because he had done no violence, neither was any deceit in his mouth." Jesus died the death of a criminal—crucified between two criminals. Yet His burial was a striking dissimilarity from that of a criminal. Jesus's burial was richly appointed, as Isaiah had prophesied.

Joseph, a member of the Sanhedrin from the town of Arimathea, was described as prominent, wealthy, good, and upright. As a member of the ruling council, Joseph had not consented to the decision to crucify Jesus. Scripture says that he was awaiting the kingdom of God, as was promised. After Jesus died around three o'clock in the afternoon, Joseph requested permission to bury the body of Jesus. Joseph, along with Nicodemus, also a member of the ruling Jewish council, took Jesus's body from the cross, wrapped His body in linen cloth, and placed His body in Joseph's own new tomb. The tomb was hewn out of rock and in a garden setting (Matthew 27). Nicodemus also assisted Joseph by bringing expensive myrrh and aloes to perfume and wrap Jesus's body, as was the custom (John 19). Joseph and Nicodemus must have worked quickly as the High Sabbath of Passover would have begun around six o'clock on the evening Jesus died.

Matthew's gospel then records an effort to secure Jesus's body.

> Now the next day … the chief priests and Pharisees came together unto Pilate, saying, "Sir, we remember that that deceiver said, while he was yet alive, 'After three days I will rise again.' Command therefore that the sepulcher be made sure until the third day, lest his disciples come by night and steal him away, and say unto the people, 'He is risen from the dead:' so the last error shall be worse than the

> first." Pilate said unto them, "Ye have a watch: go your way, make it as sure as ye can." So they went, and made the sepulcher sure, sealing the stone, and setting a watch. (Matthew 27:62–66)

Luke 8 (supported by the other gospels) reveals that as Jesus traveled from place to place in His ministry, there were several women who followed Him, helping financially or ministering to Jesus in whatever way they could. Some of these devoted women had been delivered by Jesus from evil spirits and physical infirmities. They surely experienced such great healing and deliverance that they committed their lives to following and attending to Jesus! Mary Magdalene and another Mary, Joanna, Susanna, and Salome, are listed as having observed the crucifixion, along with *many other* "women which came up with him unto Jerusalem" (Mark 15:40–41).

On the day Jesus was crucified, "The women also, which came with him from Galilee, followed after, and beheld the sepulcher, and how his body was laid. And they returned, and prepared spices and ointments" (Luke 23:55–56). This group of women was probably unaware that Jesus's body had already been properly prepared for burial by Joseph and Nicodemus. They also prepared spices and fragrant oils, which they had planned to apply to Jesus's body on

Sunday, the first day of the following week. (There were three consecutive high, holy events starting midweek when Jesus was crucified. Passover was on the fourteenth day of the month of Abib. The fifteenth was the first of seven days of the Feast of Unleavened Bread, a sacred assembly with no work. Then the Firstfruits celebration was on the sixteenth.)

One wonders whether it was tradition for women to prepare burial spiccs and to prcparc thc body for burial. It surcly seems like the type of tender sacrifice that would come from a woman's heart. God often places within the heart of women the maternal qualities of tenderness for suffering and meticulous attention in caring for all things physical. Whether or not it was considered a woman's responsibility, it was, in fact, women who fearlessly followed to see where Jesus would be buried. It was, indeed, a group of devoted women who arose early, before daylight, on the day following the weekly Sabbath to go to the tomb to anoint Jesus's body. It was the last loving-kindness they could show to their Beloved. Or so they thought!

Their efforts were rewarded, as the women were first to know the Lord had arisen. Hearts pounding, they ran to tell the apostles the tomb was empty. After the apostles had come and examined the tomb, they left and returned to their homes, not sure of what had happened to the body.

John 20 records that Mary Magdalene, however, remained at the tomb, weeping, after everyone else had left. She bent over, looked inside, and saw two angels seated where Jesus's body had been—one at the head and one at the foot. Mary Magdalene, out of whom Jesus had cast seven demons, found herself face-to-face with angels. Then, turning around and surely with a myriad of emotions, Mary was first to see the resurrected Lord.

Connecting the Dots

- Isaiah 53:11–12
- Psalm 16:9–11
- Matthew 12:39–40
- 1 Corinthians 15:20–23
- Exodus 25:16–21

The Reality of Resurrection

Bible Reading: Luke 24:36–44; John 20:24–31, 21:1–14

Without Boundaries

"Have ye here any meat?" One of the first of several post-resurrection appearances by Jesus to the apostles and followers assembled together surely produced a multitude of feelings and responses. Knowing they would need confirmation, Jesus substantiated His presence by asking for food to eat. Luke 24 says they were startled and frightened, thinking they had seen a ghost; then they quickly transitioned to amazed and joyful, as the truth became clear. Imagine seeing someone whose brutal death you witnessed suddenly appear without having entered the room through traditional means! Yet there He stood, touchable flesh, asking for food to prove and verify this reality. It was, indeed, proof of the one reality of the universe: Almighty God in all of His power and faithfulness and mercy and grace.

Another appearance to the apostles appears to have been, at least in part, for the apostle Thomas's benefit. Just one apostle with doubt was important enough to bring about the next visit to the Eleven, though several more recorded visitations occurred thereafter. These men He had mentored to spread the gospel were very important to Jesus, and their irrefutable knowledge of His resurrection was essential to the gospel they would carry to the world.

Jesus, the Creator, so completely understood the creature. He understood the fright of His emergence, so His unexpected appearances began with a comforting blessing: "Peace." He understood the weakness of human faith, so He did things to prove the reality of His presence, like eating, and inviting them to touch Him. He understood how slow we are to learn, so He taught by repetition, rehearsing over and over to the apostles the prophecy concerning His suffering, death, and resurrection.

Another of Jesus's post-resurrection appearances to the apostles is both amazing and gratifying. Jesus watched from the shore of the Sea of Galilee early one morning as some of the apostles were fishing— without success. Reminiscent of a similar event recorded in Luke 5, He instructed them where to find the fish. Jesus cooked breakfast for them that morning over an open fire—bread and the freshest of fish. "Come and dine," He said. What a wonderful experience! The beauty and promise of early morning, a warm fire, the smell of fresh food cooking, good friends! Breakfast with the Almighty by the lake! Awesome!

So loving is Jesus toward us, so compassionate and merciful! He understood our bondage to sin, and He became our righteousness. He understood our helplessness, and He became our advocate. We are like little children before Him—frail and dependent—but we can peacefully trust His love and compassion. He invites us to let Him prove Himself a reality in our lives—alive and powerful.

Connecting the Dots

- Psalm 16:9–10
- Isaiah 55:1–7

The Reality of Resurrection

Bible Reading: Luke 24:13–32

Reasoning with the Travelers

In another post-resurrection appearance, Jesus traveled *incognito* on the road to a town called Emmaus. Coming alongside of two men (Cleopas and another unnamed follower of Jesus), He asked, "What manner of communications are these that ye have one to another, as ye walk, and are sad?"

With faces downcast, they lamented, "We trusted that it had been he which should have redeemed Israel." The two followers of Jesus were speaking words of despair, words without faith or hope. Hope deferred truly makes the heart sick (Proverbs 13:12)! Humanity struggles with faith. We tend to be short-sighted, focusing only on our current circumstances and what we have determined, often mistakenly, to be our immediate needs. How foolish we are, and slow to believe what has been spoken (Luke 24:25)!

Earlier Jesus had said, "The Son of Man must suffer … and be rejected of the elders and chief priests and scribes, and be slain, and be raised the third day" (Luke 9:22). He had explained it all many times and in no uncertain terms; but as Satan would have it, their hopes were dashed and their words had become faithless. As they traveled along together

He reminded them with Scripture, "And beginning at Moses and all the Prophets, he expounded unto them in all the scriptures the things concerning himself" (Luke 24:27).

> For it became him, for whom are all things, and by whom are all things, in bringing many sons unto glory, to make the captain of their salvation perfect through sufferings. Forasmuch then as the children are partakers of flesh and blood, he also himself likewise took part of the same; that through death he might destroy him that had the power of death … It behoved [was needful and proper for] him to be made like unto his brethren, that he might be a merciful and faithful high priest in things pertaining to God, to make reconciliation for the sins of the people. (Hebrews 2:10, 14, 17)

Certainly the Christ had to suffer! Slain from the creation of the world (Revelation 13:8), His persona, His destiny, and His triumph were revealed by God through the ancient prophets.

Undeniably the Christ was resurrected! From prophecy to firsthand accounts recorded in the gospels, this we believe.

> [Luke wrote about] all that Jesus began both to do and teach until the day in which he was

> taken up [to heaven], after that he through the Holy Ghost had given commandments unto the apostles whom he had chosen: To whom also he shewed himself alive after his passion by many infallible proofs, being seen of them forty days, and speaking of the things pertaining to the kingdom of God. (Acts 1:1–3)

Without a doubt Christ has ascended back to the Father! This is how we know: Before His crucifixion, He told His apostles He would not leave them as orphans, but God the Father would send them the Holy Spirit to comfort and counsel them. After the resurrection, in the presence of the apostles, Jesus ascended, was enveloped in a cloud, and disappeared into the sky. Ten days later the Holy Spirit came with a powerful entrance. Still present in the world today, He is the spirit presence of Almighty God, drawing those He would to Christ, guiding and comforting all who would be filled by Him. The Spirit is our witness today to the resurrection and ascension of Christ. Thanks be to God!

By the end of their encounter, the two followers of Jesus exclaimed in realization, "Did not our heart burn within us, while he talked with us by the way, and while he opened to us the scriptures?" (Luke 24:32).

Resurrection Appearances

- Matthew 28
- Mark 16
- Luke 24
- John 20–21
- Acts 1

Part 7

Looking Forward from the Past

Introduction

Final Instruction

[Jesus], being assembled together with [His followers], commanded them that they should not depart from Jerusalem, "but wait for the promise of the Father, which... ye have heard of me. For John truly baptized with water; but ye shall be baptized with the Holy Ghost not many days hence... ye shall receive power after that the Holy Ghost is come upon you: and ye shall be witnesses unto me both in Jerusalem and in all Judaea, and in Samaria, and unto the uttermost part of the earth." And when he had spoken these things, while they beheld, he was taken up; and a cloud received him out of their sight. And while they looked stedfastly toward heaven as he went up, behold, two men stood by them in white apparel; which also said, "Ye men of Galilee, why stand ye gazing up into heaven? This same Jesus, which is taken up from you

> into heaven, shall so come in like manner as ye have seen him go into heaven." (Acts 1:4–11)

Again, Jesus's instructions were *first*, do "not depart from Jerusalem… wait for the promise… ye shall be baptized with the Holy Ghost." *Then*, "ye shall receive power, after that the Holy Ghost is come upon you." And *finally*, "ye shall be witnesses unto me… unto the uttermost part of the earth."

Matthew, Mark, and Luke record that when Jesus was about to leave the earth forty days after the resurrection, He gave His followers instruction and then visibly ascended into heaven. Mark's gospel, (12:35–37) reveals understanding of David's prophetic words in Psalm 110 and those of Jesus (Luke 22:69), confirming that the Christ would then take His place enthroned next to God the Father. We know not only where He went but also what He is doing.

> But this man [Jesus Christ], because he continueth ever, hath an unchangeable priesthood. Wherefore he is able also to save them to the uttermost that come unto God by him, seeing *he ever liveth to make intercession* for them. For such an high priest became us, who is holy, harmless, undefiled, separate from sinners, and made higher than the heavens. (Hebrews 7:24–26)

Looking Forward from the Past

Bible Reading: Luke 24:49; Acts 1:1–5; Acts 2:1–18

Holy Spirit Baptism

Scripture heralds the Holy Trinity: one Supreme Being (monotheism) who is omnipotent, omnipresent, omniscient, and eternal, comprised of the threefold *personalities* of the Father, Son, and Holy Spirit. Truly the greatness of God cannot be defined and explained by mortal, earthly man! Father, Son, and Spirit being One, they are always in agreement. As the Son of God carried out the will of God the Father, so the Holy Spirit also executes the will of the Father. The unlimited power of the Almighty is present in the Father, Son, and Spirit.

The Holy Spirit of God is a component in all of scripture and all of human existence. In scripture the Holy Spirit is often referred to as "Spirit of God," but we also read of the Spirit in symbolism (i.e., fire, oil, water, wind, dove, cloud). The Holy Spirit is first recognized in Genesis 1. God's universe, including earth, was dark and empty, and the Spirit of God hovered over the waters that covered earth. The Holy Spirit was present and participated in creation (Genesis 1:26). The Holy Spirit is referenced throughout the Bible, from that first chapter of Genesis to the last chapter of Revelation in verse

17, where we read His invitation for all to come and receive Christ.

Scripture records that the Holy Spirit was responsible for executing, enabling, and empowering miraculous exploits. We will not nearly skim the surface here, but note the diverse and unlimited power of the Spirit. For a few examples from the Old Testament, in Exodus 31 God filled a man named Bezaleel with the Spirit of God, enabling him with knowledge, skills, and talents in artistic crafts. God used this man to create the high and holy artifacts of the tent of meeting and the ark of the testimony used in the Jewish tabernacle. In the book of Numbers, Joshua, described as "a man in whom is the Spirit," was chosen to succeed the great and humble Moses and serve as leader of (possibly) several million Jews. In Judges 6–7, a man named Gideon was empowered by the Holy Spirit to defeat an army of thousands with only three hundred men. The Holy Spirit lifted and carried the prophet Ezekiel into visions, giving revelation of the future.

In the New Testament, the Virgin Mary was impregnated with the Son of God in human form by the miraculous work of the Holy Spirit (Luke 1). When John the Baptist baptized Jesus, the Holy Spirit came in the form of a dove and descended upon Jesus (Luke 3). Isaiah had prophesied of Jesus that the Spirit would rest on Him in the form of wisdom and understanding, counsel and power, knowledge and fear of the Lord (Isaiah 11).

The followers of Christ were admonished by Jesus before He ascended to the Father to wait in Jerusalem for this gift of the Holy Spirit's baptism and infilling (John 14:17; Acts 1:5). On the festival day of Pentecost, ten days after Jesus had ascended back to heaven, the believers were all together, possibly in an upper room associated with the temple where they daily met for prayer (Acts 2:46). They were praying in agreement and with expectancy as they obediently awaited the promise of the coming Counselor. One doubts that they fully knew what to expect in regard to the Counselor's arrival and infilling. When the promised Holy Spirit came, it was a powerful entrance that would not have gone without notice. There was a very loud sound like a violent wind. In fact, when those who were in Jerusalem for the Pentecost festival (Feast of Weeks) "heard the sound," a crowd came together to investigate the phenomenon. The crowd was even more bewildered because each of them heard the group of local Christians speaking, not in their native language, but in the various languages of those present from other parts of the world. Fire appeared among those being filled by the Spirit and came to rest above the heads of each one who was awaiting His arrival.

We know the Spirit was already involved in the lives of those He filled that day. Jesus acknowledged that His followers knew the Spirit, because the Spirit was *with* them (John 14:17). It is the Spirit that helps humankind recognize Jesus as the Savior and draws sinners to Him. The difference would be a powerful *infilling* that would allow the Spirit to live in our hearts and minds and souls to guide our thoughts and actions. Following that great outpouring in Acts 2, we can look into the New Testament and see the Spirit at work.

Examples in the New Testament include more miraculous workings of the Spirit. In Acts, the Spirit instructed the apostle Philip to approach a chariot wherein an Ethiopian official was reading from Isaiah. The man from Ethiopia accepted Christ and was baptized by Philip that day. Acts 8:39 records, "When they came up out of the water, the Spirit of the Lord [suddenly] caught away Philip, that the eunuch saw him no more." (Philip, however, re-appeared some twenty miles away!) The renowned apostle Paul was redirected and not allowed to preach in certain places at certain times (i.e., Acts 16:6–10) by the omniscient Holy Spirit's leadership. For one more illustration, in the book of Revelation (1:10), the apostle John was taken by the Holy Spirit into the future to witness and record events that are yet to come. John was also taken into the throne room of God in heaven (Revelation 4)! Over and over the Spirit of God appears throughout the

Old and New Testaments to empower those who would be used by God.

From a more personal perspective, the Holy Spirit's presence within an individual is an intimate and fervent experience. He fills every fiber of one's being with love and comfort and constant companionship. He comes and enters our souls, bearing spiritual gifts (1 Corinthians 12–14). Being full of God's Spirit is the perfect plan for strengthening and blessing believers. Every thought and every feeling we experience is known to the Spirit, and His function is to comfort, counsel, and conform our thoughts to the will of Christ. He, along with Jesus, feels our burdens and intercedes to the Father on our behalf. Stop for a personal moment and recall your heaviest burden ever carried or deepest spirit wound ever experienced. Some burdens are so crushing that we cannot speak of them. Scripture describes that the Holy Spirit helps us in our weaknesses, and when "we know not what we should pray for as we ought … the [omniscient] Spirit itself maketh intercession for us" (Romans 8:26). Truly, He feels what we feel! "He that searcheth the hearts knoweth what is the mind of the Spirit, because [the Spirit] maketh intercession for the saints according to the will of God" (Romans 8:27).

The Spirit can reveal to us the will of God! Jesus said, "The Comforter, which is the Holy Ghost, whom the Father will send in my name, he shall teach you all things, and bring all things to your remembrance, whatsoever I have said unto you" (John 14:26). The Spirit "will guide you into all truth … shew you things to come … glorify [Jesus]" (John 16:13–14). How awesome! God our Creator, so thoroughly loving us, constantly communicating in every thought, every breath, every physical movement! Oh, the beauty of that kind of relationship with the Almighty!

Oh, that we might live so that every thought is taken captive and made to conform to God's will! Would that every word we speak is inspired and directed by the Holy Spirit! This should be our highest aspiration as Christians: God literally filling us with Himself for confirmation, direction, productivity, and comfort. That requires our constant attention and complete submission to the Spirit.

God is always faithful to do what He promises (2 Corinthians 1:20). He promised to send the Holy Spirit to live in the hearts, souls, and minds of individuals, and the Spirit has indeed come.

Connecting the Dots

- Deuteronomy 6:4
- Luke 11:9–13
- John 1:32–33

- Matthew 12:31–32
- For further study: Fire: Exodus 13:21; Acts 2:3. Cloud: Exodus 16:10; Water: John 7:38–39; Wind: Acts 2:2

Looking Forward from the Past

Bible Readings: Acts 1:1–11; Matthew 28:18–20; Luke 12:31

Perpetuating the Kingdom

The very last directive spoken by Jesus before His ascension was for His disciples to preach the gospel to all nations, sharing what they knew about Jesus as Savior. More than a vocation, this directive was to be an authorized kingdom appointment with empowerment—kingdom ambassadors. For perspective, all of the admonitions given by Jesus at the last supper were instruction in how to accomplish this final imperative, along with comfort and encouragement for the difficulty of the task.

A look into their future reveals that the admonition from Jesus during the meal was effective. The Acts of the Apostles chronicled several decades of the spread of the gospel of Christ. The apostles, having been convinced that Jesus was the Messiah, wholeheartedly and fervently accepted the mandate of the Great Commission given by Jesus. They started in Jerusalem, and along with Paul and others who accepted Christ, they set out to evangelize the world.

Evident in Acts are the attitudes and qualities of Jesus in the lives of the apostles and many of their converts. Having been filled with the Holy Spirit, they were empowered to witness, preach, and live the gospel with boldness. Jesus was faithful to honor their obedience with miraculous answers to prayer. They served their fellowman with gifts, offerings, and the work of their hands, sharing all they had. They sincerely loved and fellowshipped with other believers with glad hearts. They humbly endured scorn, persecution, and even death for their message. All of this was as Jesus had commanded.

Jesus's followers had fully grasped the concept of the kingdom of God that He had taught them. They realized that the kingdom heralded by John the Baptist (Luke 3) had indeed emerged upon earth with the advent of Christ. They understood that hardship would be necessary to help bring about the kingdom in their lives and the lives of others, and that the kingdom is worth all sacrifice. They understood that the kingdom would grow and expand not only to the Jews, but also to the Gentiles, and their responsibility would be to spread the word. They knew that helping to bring about the kingdom on earth secured for them an eternal future in the kingdom in heaven with God. Their message to others was to live lives worthy of the kingdom (1 Thessalonians 2:11–12; Ephesians 4:1–3).

How could we possibly do less! That same directive from Matthew 28 that Jesus gave to the apostles is a command to all who would receive Christ, from the time of Acts to the present. When we realize that eternity is a reality and that heaven and hell are the only two options, we should feel constrained to share that knowledge and the saving message of Christ with all who will listen. As witnesses for Christ, we carry the kingdom in our hearts until such time as the kingdom comes finally and permanently to earth (Luke 17:20–22). We must remember that our witness is a mandate (Matthew 10:32; Romans 10:9).

To be effective witnesses for Christ, we must consider ourselves to be official ambassadors of the kingdom of God. When nations around the world make the effort to have diplomatic relations with other countries, they often send an ambassador to live in their embassies abroad. Those ambassadors develop relationships with the host nation by representing their own nation as excellent and worthy of alliance. In the best interest of a nation sending a representative, ambassadors are chosen carefully from the brightest and best, as they will be the living human impression of their home nation. As ambassadors for the kingdom of God, we have the solemn responsibility to represent Christ.

International ambassadors must live with integrity—above reproach. They must be wise, personable, hospitable, and gracious. Ambassadors of the kingdom of God must do likewise. Christ's ambassadors must not be offensive in any way (1 Corinthians 10:32; 2 Corinthians 6:3), yet we must faithfully declare truth. The love of Christ visible in and through us to others will help to accomplish this complex task.

International ambassadors must have a thorough understanding of how their countries function (i.e., US constitutional law), as well as understand the government of the country they will be serving. From a spiritual perspective, having been born into sin, we all understand the carnal mindset. Our personal experience before accepting Christ is, in itself, an education in how to approach the unsaved to present and clearly define the kingdom of God. Further, we also understand and can identify with the challenges of committing our lives to Christ (Acts 14:22). We must seek God's guidance and wisdom and study His Word as to how to share that truth (1 Peter 3:15–16).

International ambassadors must have excellent communication skills, as war and peace can hinge on a word. As exemplary ambassadors for Christ and the kingdom of God, we should study God's laws and be prepared to answer questions concerning the kingdom we represent (2 Timothy 2:15). We should pray for God's help in presenting His eternal kingdom to others with love, grace, clarity, and passion. However, any simple, sincere, and loving attempt to win others to Christ will be honored by Him. To quote an old hymn, "With deeds of love and mercy the heavenly kingdom comes."[3] Those to whom we represent Christ must sense in our spirits His gentleness and humility, a true indication of excellence.

> Our Father in heaven, may Your name be hallowed in our hearts. Your kingdom come, Your will be done in earth, just as it is in heaven (Matthew 6). Your kingdom come and Your will be done in our hearts and in our homes. Help us to live our lives worthy of God's calling and kingdom.

Connecting the Dots

- 2 Corinthians 5:16–20
- Matthew 10:37–38

---

[3] "Lead On, O King Eternal," Ernest W. Shurtleff (Public Domain)

Part 8

In Conclusion

Bible Reading: John 3:14–18; Matthew 24; Revelation 22

Now That We Know

Eternity is a concept understood since Adam and Eve were in the Garden of Eden. (Remember the tree of life from Genesis 2:9?) Abraham understood that the Lord is the eternal God (Genesis 21:33). God spoke through Isaiah that He would make Israel an eternal excellency (Isaiah 60:15). Paul wrote to the Ephesians that God's eternal purpose was accomplished in Jesus Christ.

Time, however, is not eternal. Old Testament prophets revealed events of the future that we now read as history. They also revealed things we have yet to see. Some Old Testament prophets gave detailed descriptions of events approaching the end of time (e.g., Daniel 11–12; Ezekiel 38–39). Jacob, Isaiah, Micah (Old Testament), Jesus, Luke, Paul, James, and Peter (New Testament) spoke and wrote about "the last days," confirmation that time is not eternal.

Late in His ministry, the apostles came to Jesus with a serious question about the future. "Tell us… what shall be the sign of thy coming, and of the end of the world [dispensation]" (Matthew 24:3). Jesus's answer to their question is sobering (Matthew 24, Mark 13, Luke 21). Some of what He said we may not thoroughly understand until it takes place. Yet we feel comforted and protected when we belong to Him and are covered by His cleansing blood. He encourages us, "When these things begin to come to pass, then look up, and lift up your heads; for your redemption draweth nigh" (Luke 21:28). We remember again His promise from John 14:2–3: "I will come again, and receive you unto myself; that where I am, there ye may be also."

As we read the description Jesus revealed to the apostles concerning the end of the age, perhaps we may sense in our hearts with the Holy Spirit confirming that we are nearing the "last days" of time. Understanding the unsettling circumstances of the present constrains us to examine our relationship with Jesus.

Now that we know that Jesus is the Son of God, how should we respond to His great sacrifice? We should confess our sin and ask forgiveness, thereby receiving salvation and eternal life. As 1 John 1:9 says, "If we confess our sins, he is faithful and just to forgive us our sins." "Blessed is he whose transgression is forgiven, whose sin is covered … in whose spirit there is no guile" (Psalm 32:1–2).

Now that we know that our every spiritual need has been met through Jesus Christ, how are we helped by this knowledge? We are empowered. "When I cried thou answeredst … strengthenedst me" (Psalm 138:3). As the apostle Paul wrote to Timothy, God gives us "a spirit … of power, and of love and of a sound mind" (2 Timothy 1:7).

Now that we know the Holy Spirit has been sent to help us, what should we do? We must welcome His indwelling and commit to His leadership in our lives. "Then said Jesus to them, 'Peace be unto you: as my Father has sent me, even so send I you.' And when he had said this, he breathed on them, and saith unto them, 'Receive ye the Holy Ghost'" (John 20:21–22).

Now that we know how we should live, what purpose should our lives serve? Our lives should glorify God. "Ye are a chosen generation, a royal priesthood, an holy nation, a peculiar people; that ye should shew forth the praises of him who hath called you out of darkness into his marvelous light" (1 Peter 2:9).

Now that we know what Jesus did for us, what should we be doing for Him? We should obey the Great Commission (Matthew 28:19–20), spreading the gospel of Jesus Christ.

> God was in Christ, reconciling the world unto himself, not imputing their trespasses unto them; and hath committed unto *us* the word of reconciliation. Now then we are ambassadors for Christ, as though God did beseech you by us. (2 Corinthians 5:19–20)

Now that we know the reality of eternity, how can we prepare? We must be informed, alert, and ready to meet Jesus when He calls for us or returns for us.

> Watch therefore: for ye know not what hour your Lord doth come. (Matthew 24:42).
>
> The Lord is not slack concerning his promise, as some men count slackness; but is longsuffering to us-ward, not willing that any should perish, but that all should come to repentance. But the day of the Lord will come as a thief in the night. (2 Peter 3:9–10)
>
> Behold, I shew you a mystery … The trumpet shall sound, and the dead shall be raised incorruptible, and we shall be changed. (1 Corinthians 15:51–52)

Connecting the Dots

- Jeremiah 30:1–3
- Isaiah 65:17–19
- Zechariah 14:9
- Habakkuk 2:2–3

Printed and bound by PG in the USA